Claus Birkholz

Young and Dirac
The Prophets of New Physics

Are we prepared to face the new facts?

Copyright: © 2019 Claus Birkholz
Approved: 2019-08-05

Proofreading: Ole Jürgens and Ralph Hickok – www.textcelsior.de
Layout: Erik Kinting – www.buchlektorat.net

Publisher: tredition GmbH, Hamburg

978-3-7497-2476-5 (Paperback)
978-3-7497-2477-2 (Hardcover)
978-3-7497-2478-9 (e-Book)

Auch auf Deutsch erhältlich:
978-3-7497-2473-4 (Paperback)
978-3-7497-2474-1 (Hardcover)
978-3-7497-2475-8 (e-Book)

Contents

The Theory

The Story

The Theory

1. Free Will and Reproducibility

Electrodynamics once paved the way to **Special Relativity**. Einstein's merit was to introduce the **curvilinear metric** into his **General Relativity** (GR). Cosmologists had to accept meanwhile that GR might instead have been a flash in the pan (cosmic inflation decoupled from relativity, no dark energy, no dark matter, etc.). The true pioneers might have been the mathematician A. **Young** and the fundamental theorist **Dirac**, both of them busy at Cambridge.

Schrödinger stands for classical quantum *mechanics*, and not for **Quantum Gravity**, which denotes the unification of Planck's quanta with Einstein's *General* Relativity. For insiders, the battle was more about Bell's "**hidden variables**". In 1936, Podolsky, Einstein, and Rosen had postulated them in order:

1) to overcome the problem of a "collapsing wave equation" in the **measuring process** of quantum theories,
2) to override Einstein's "spooky action at a distance", which is known as "**entanglement**".

Entanglement denotes the situation that a coupled system preserves its quantum coupling *without any time delay*, irrespectively of, then, overriding the speed of light. That clearly violates the limitations expected from **causality**. Einstein's idea had been that his General Relativity might be incomplete; hidden variables could be an escape strategy. In 1964, however, the Irish physicist Bell published his no-go theorems telling us that hidden variables are *not* the solution to those problems.

Since that time, Bell's no-go theorems have conquered fundamental physics. Every theoretician proudly claims the non-existence of hidden variables in quantum systems quite generally. That opinion spread like a plague. Everybody who still dared to raise an objection quickly experienced the worldwide power of the big scientific lobby: Nobody took him seriously any more. Thus, even Einstein became marginalised post hoc.

The irony, however, was that Einstein turned out to be correct, after all! For, Bell himself admitted in a 1985 BBC television report that his no-go theorems were crucially based on his tacit assumption that there existed in nature something like **free will**. Without free will, however, his theorems faded to nothing.

Bell called the result thus corrected and replacing his no-go theorems an "absolute determinism" or, shorter, a "**superdeterminism**". According to that superdeterminism, everything should be uniquely predestined and unchangeable for all times: There should be some general consistency condition embracing the entire world without any exception.

This meant an open declaration of war towards our western civilization as it has grown over thousands of years. Just think of our jurisdiction and its sanctions against crime. Provided everything has been predetermined already, then the accused would be innocent – the culprit would be the superdeterministic combination of events our forefathers once had declared to be a crime! This, however, mistakenly asserts that those sanctions irrevocably are part of that superdeterminism, as well.

As a result, nobody took Bell's 1985 insights seriously. Instead, his outdated no-go theorems went on flourishing until today. This is supported by the purely technical fact that Bell's BBC-interview is hardly suitable to be quoted by an official journal. In our present world, remarkably, a *subjective* rumour once hastily fixed by the official opinion leaders outweighs any future *objective* correction. Hence, up to now, almost nobody dared the loss of face required to apply superdeterminism to particle physics or to cosmology.

Theoretical physics is defined as the mapping of (parts of) nature into mathematics. We only perceive what our **senses** are telling us.

But they might tell us nonsense, as well. Serious physicists, hence, only accept what can be reproduced unambiguously. The main trait is the **reproducibility** of physical results. This is its distinction from religion, which works with irreproducible "miracles".

Thus, it is amusing that the existence of something like a "free will" has been able to stay upright that long, although its implications clearly are *not* reproducible. For this reason alone, it is surprising that *in physics* the hypothesis of a "free will" could have formed at all and then also be preserved for so long.

2. Finiteness and Atomism

Another feature of physics is its atomistic nature detected by Planck when he was working at his black-body radiation law in 1900. Even before, ancient Greek philosophers already had speculated about it. This **atomism**, however, should be evident to every layman, indeed. For, nobody can count up to infinity. In physics, hence, everything must stay finite in order that we are able to keep the survey over it and can describe it in a unique way. Without a unique description, however, reproducibility hardly can be checked!

Finiteness, when extended to systems of real numbers, teaches us that fundamental physics only admits **rational numbers** because irrational numbers need an infinite number of (non-repeating) decimal digits. A finite set of elements, however, can be separated and counted. This yields the above atomistic structure in terms of "**quanta**".

Classical physics denies that atomism. Classical physics is assumed to be continuous. For continuous systems, the infinitesimal calculus was invented. The mechanistic view of our world has been thriving with it for centuries. And people are trying to keep it upright still today. Schrödinger's continuous wave equation exemplifies the resistance with which disciples of that mechanistic view of our world still actually face Planck's discrete quantum view.

Now, a continuous description might also be interpreted as the limiting case of a superposition of discrete features. This is the wave aspect of **statistics**. But don't turn a blind eye to the fact that smoothed statistics are the result of a *limiting* process, which tacitly includes the extrapolation towards an *infinite* number of elements! That extrapolation means indirectly taking into consideration additional elements that are not present there from the beginning.

Those "**hidden variables**", of course, are unphysical, ambiguous, pure fantasy. You could choose them however you like. They are what Bell's no-go theorems are <u>ex</u>cluding for combining causality with entanglement. Their <u>in</u>clusion, however, is the source for a **macroscopic** extension of a basically microscopic world.

Let us keep in mind: A macroscopic description contains more parameters than experimentally measured! A quantum theory describes the microscopic situation, where there is just 1 state and 1 ("diagonal") measurable direction. The macroscopic view, however, is less exact: The result of measuring some state A – say at a position z – might be some state B – say at a position z'. Provided the difference $z'-z$, now, is negligibly small with respect to the absolute value z, its measuring result could *approximately* be equal to z, and B, then, could "approximately" equal A. Without having quantised spacetime, hence, we have to expect that an entire spectrum of values B will be (mis)interpreted exactly to be =A – with all its curious implications for a theory to be accepted then or not.

According to Bell's words, those microscopic deviations are "hidden" with respect to the macroscopic world – disguising the fact that the final state B is <u>not *exactly*</u> equal to the initial state A. Thus, the macroscopic world is working with **approximation**s manifesting themselves in terms of (reducible or even irreducible) **superpositions** of a great number of states *almost* coinciding.

This new definition of what is "**macroscopic**" according to Bell's superdeterminism is the most important feature of New Physics. It cannot be underestimated! Planck's summation of a finite number of <u>discrete</u> quanta replacing their <u>continuous</u> integration is the key to that problem. By his method of firing the singularities inherent in classical potentials like those of Yukawa or Coulomb-type applications, singular models of classical literature are unexpectedly becoming finite and simple. In their discrete forms, <u>Yukawa or even Coulomb potentials might result in a non-singular way</u>.

3. Faster than Light

According to Pythagoras, a (squared) distance is measured by adding the squares of its components. In 2 dimensions that distance defines the radius of a circle (or, when stretched, the principal axes of an ellipse), in more dimensions a sphere (or an ellipsoid).

Now, Einstein demonstrated that, in order correctly to describe Maxwell's electrodynamics, the time direction has to be multiplied by the imaginary unit, in addition – which is not present in his 3 space directions. When inserted into Pythagoras, this squared imaginary unit will effectively switch the positive sign of its squared time component to a negative sign. The result is **Special Relativity**.

This sign switch in the time direction transforms Pythagoras' circle (or sphere) to a hyperbola (or hyperboloid, respectively). Contrary to a circle or an ellipse, a hyperbola, however, has 2 separate branches that do not touch each other. This transformation from a compact circle or ellipse to a non-compact hyperbola, triggered by that sign switch, thus:

1. rips the original circle or ellipse into 2 pieces,
2. stretches and squeezes the rest.

In physics, the (negative) density gradient of a point distribution designates a "force". On the homogeneous surface of a sphere, where all positions are equivalent, the point concentration should be distributed equally. A point-by-point transformation of this sphere to a hyperboloid – which is a mere exercise for a mathematician – will yield a density distribution there that is definitely non-uniform.

On the hyperboloid, hence, **(geometrical) forces** will be created that are absent from the original sphere! And those forces will become extreme (velocity of light) at those locations where our original figure is torn to pieces.

When keeping some of the coordinates fixed while letting the remaining ones change, the total set of points, depending on those fixed values, will be sliced into sections that are orthogonal to each other. But each of those coordinate systems will slice the complete set of points in a different way (cf. the red vs. the green way):

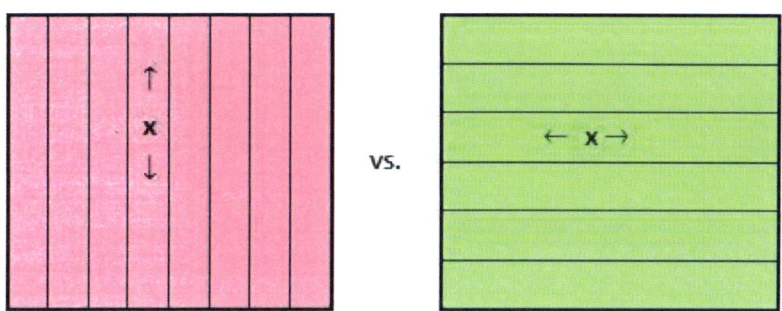

In classical physics both slicing schemes would be related by an r-number formula (giving the same quantised _real_ "Lie algebra" – whatever this might be); in Quantum Gravity (QG), however, the relation will be given by a c-number formula (giving the same "_complex_ Lie algebra"). Thus the point is: QG is distinguishing the compact, "**closed**" representation by the "**reaction channel**" from its (formally) non-compact, i.e., "**open**" representation by the "**dynamic channel**".

In both cases, the "points" represented by these "channels" may be designated as (the expectation values of) "**generators**" because we are treating Quantum Gravity here, contrary to classical physics, as a thoroughly quantised model; quantum _mechanics_ and Einstein's _General_ Relativity are just limiting models reflecting classical physics.

Because both channels describe the same set of points, the finiteness constraint of our closed reaction channel is automatically transferred to the dynamic channel, as well. Its infinite, asymptotic na-

13

ture, thus, proves to be <u>cut off</u> somewhere. In physics this means: That **"pseudo**-open" dynamic channel will have to be represented by *<u>finite</u>-dimensional representations,* as well!

Classical physics works with *in*finite representations, instead. Many of its technical problems arise from those unphysical, infinite singularities that are neither needed nor observable. Quantum Gravity avoids them from the start. Clearly, it is hard work trying to persuade the elder generation to abandon the technical prejudices they have cultivated and expanded for so long. Their international lobby is preventing QG from gaining a proper foothold in science – in spite of its breath-taking experimental success.

Dynamics, hence, is bounded. Contrary to the case of classical physics, there are no singularities. This does not mean that our universe is bounded by some rim we could knock at. A better picture would be that our point distribution is thinning out more and more towards some imaginary limit. And somewhere we are passing its last point without observing that there will be no more point behind.

Probability amplitudes are summed up according to Pythagoras. The **"conservation of probability"** postulated by physicists, hence, is a property of the reaction channel. Likewise, entanglement is working in the reaction channel. On the other hand, dynamics is a manifestation of the dynamic channel, and causality is a property defined by dynamics. In classical physics, both channels are identified with each other. Bell's no-go theorem is based on this identification.

In the above sketch, however, point x cannot simultaneously march into the red, vertical direction <u>and</u> into the green, horizontal direction. Although the full red domain is equal to its full green counterpart, those individual *slices* denoting probability conservation in the reaction channel and lack of dynamical motion in the dynamic channel are *not* identical – as classical physics tacitly assumes. But this contradiction is exactly the source of Bell's no-go theorems.

In QG, both channels can be *expanded* into each other! Thus, Bell's contradiction disappears: causality and entanglement are both true side by side. Only, both channels are *not commeasurable* with each other! (Just compare it with the spin components.)

4. Historical Background

Before 1900, physics was still a hotchpotch of individual disciplines, all more or less independent of each other. In the course of the 20th century, a melting process started. Even chemistry turned out just to be a combination of quantum mechanics with thermodynamics. Biology and medicine, however, still resisted any unification.

Physics then went from being regarded as an outcome of the **variational principle**, which is intimately related to the Lagrangian model. Both of them had been developed in the 18th century. The variational principle had become the highlight of treating mechanical problems. In mathematics, **Lagrangian formalism** is based on the non-discrete, <u>continuous</u> "functional analysis of many variables". Their property to subordinate all that might happen under just <u>one single parameter</u> is crucial.

In physics, time is usually chosen as this 1 parameter. Even those notorious "string models" admit just one "time-like" dimension only, while all remaining dimensions are demanded to be "space-like". We shall observe, however, that this restriction will turn out to be too stringent for physics.

The 20th century spectacularly started with Planck's introduction of discrete "quanta" replacing continuous structures, followed by Einstein's relativity theories. Both models, that of relativity and that of quantum theories, rapidly continued to develop to complete "**field theories**". Even quantum theories still used that giant machinery of a *continuous* functional analysis for dealing with the *discrete* problems of quanta, cf. Schrödinger's method.

Thus, the world of physicists proved not yet to be mature for QG: The requirements of the variational principle and of the Lagrangian formalism prevented the unification of quantum theory with Einstein's *General* Relativity. Its main obstacle had been that **duality** not understood between the **dynamic** and the **reaction channel**.

The preceding chapter has been dedicated to stripping that un-justified restriction off fundamental physics by redefining physics to be based on what mathematicians would denote as a **model of generators**. *(Their "complex Lie algebra" is the highest common denominator of both channels. And a generator is represented by a square matrix. More about this later.)*

In n dimensions, the n *diagonal* entries of a matrix are commeasurable. This is the **microscopic view** of physics. The **macroscopic view**, however, is an application of the law of great numbers resorting to superpositions. We shall still observe that all n x n generators of an nxn-matrix representing a generator can be made *approximately* commeasurable by applying appropriate statistics.

Such results derive from the mathematical discipline of "**group theory**". Spin is a notion of group theory, too. Einstein did not like group theory. Hence, his General Relativity does not incorporate spin; for GR, **spin** is an "alien". In group theory, however, spin is one of its fundamental properties. This might be another obstacle preventing both theories from being united successfully, so far.

The main notion in group theory, however, is "**irreducibility**", telling us which combination of quanta belong together in order to build up a particle, e.g., and which does not. Like spin, this notion that is important for group theory has not been used by Einstein in his GR.

On the other hand, that "irreducibility" is the basic notion allowing us to write down the "**world formula**". Hence Einstein never was able to write it down. For, the invariants of group theory are just *defined* by that irreducibility; they are called "**Casimir operators**" there (to be presented later). Einstein's "world formula for every Casimir existing, must read

$$\text{Casimir} = \text{const.}$$

5. Quantum Gravity

Let me briefly summarise what we have found already to be of importance for Quantum Gravity:

- **Reproducibility** needs Bell's <u>superdeterminism</u>. This prevents a *free will*.
- **Finiteness** yields an <u>atomistic</u> world with *no (non-recoverable) singularities*.
- A *complex* **Lie algebra** yields the duality between the 2 channels, providing the coexistence of <u>causality</u> and <u>entanglement</u>.
- Geometrical <u>forces</u> are the result of relating the **secondary dynamic channel** to the **primary reaction channel**.
- **Statistics**, by the *"law of great numbers"* is adding the <u>macroscopic view</u> of physics to its primary *microscopic view*.

Further implications are:

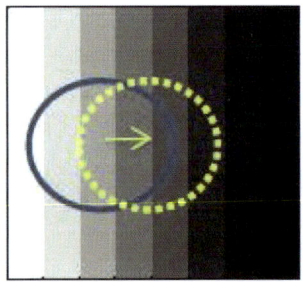

- Triggered by the gradient of probability, **motion**, then, means hopping from one fixed-time slice to the next one. *(In polar coordinates these would be time shells.)*

Our 2 channels are not commeasurable with each other. Compare this case with Wheeler-deWitt's oversimplified trial not to <u>solve</u> the Gordian knot of but to <u>cut</u> it by brute force: They are completely banning *any* time-dependence from theory. For, they had correctly found that an exact measurement of time trivially would have prevented time from varying – our slicing scheme with respect to time.

Because of their tacit identification of both channels, however, their model was doomed to end up in a disaster: *Functional analysis is no good guide for handling the discrete quantum structure of physics!* What they had been doing was throwing the baby out with the bath water.

Statistics also provide probability. A normalisable probability (number of accepted cases divided by the number of all cases) needs a division operator. Now, number theory teaches us that a system of numbers accepting a division operator has a dimension 2 to the power of n where n is not greater than 3. (For r-numbers, n=0, for c-numbers, n=1.) From experiment we learn that all $2**3 = 8$ dimensions are needed, indeed. Hence:

- The basic **dimension** of Quantum Gravity **is** fixed to be **= 8**.

In order to unify Planck's world of quanta with Einstein's General Relativity, the objective of Quantum Gravity is it to describe elementary particles and our cosmos by the same set of equations; only the values of their numerical constants should differ. By them, a Quantum Gravity necessarily will contain **external parameters**, in addition, which itself ca<u>nnot</u> predict in advance. Our universe, hence, turns out to be some subordinate partial subsystem which – howsoever – will be **embedded in some higher system** fixing those parameters, a system which, therefore, might possibly obey different axioms.

6. Generators and Metric

Attention: For a *deeper* understanding of physics, regrettably, this chapter is somewhat mathematical. Nevertheless, people who are not sure what all this might mean, should not give up, anyway.

Einstein already used tensors in fundamental physics. His General Relativity is a model based on tensors. Within a continuous framework, the mathematical discipline of tensors is **differential geometry**; in a discrete one it is **group theory**. Tensors are multiple vectors, i.e., they are based on (Kronecker) products of vectors in some linear *superposition* such that the final tensor cannot usually be split into just *two* vectors as factors.

Hence a tensor is fitted with several vector labels. Group theory classifies them according to symmetry classes (Young tableaux). In a physical interpretation, vectors come across in 2 types: a **contravariant** vector (lower label) serves as an input, a **covariant** vector (upper label) as the output of some reaction (or v.v.).

(But observe the ambiguity of the notion "contravariant"! The apparently paradoxical formulation reads that a label which, in some fixed situation, is identified to be <u>covariant</u> in some relative situation is designated to be <u>contravariant</u> to a certain different vector identified to be contravariant.)

Tensors also might simultaneously be fitted with labels of both types; for example:
$$T_a{}^b = \Sigma_{vw} \, v_a w^b \, .$$

Only, by its "**2nd quantisation**" particle physics does not respect the clean gap between input and output issues. As a direct consequence of this mathematical inconsistency, all attempts towards a "unification of field theories" have turned out to be in vain since Dirac in the 1930s; they are still actually stagnating. The reason is that that formalism undermines the conservation of quanta as individually conserved entities:

The **vacuum** stopped being empty, particles went to be created in pairs out of nothing and disappeared, there, again! The two powerful obstacles on the trail towards constructing a Quantum Gravity, hence, are 2nd quantisation on the hand of particle physics, and the ignorance of irreducibility on the hand of General Relativity.

Bilinear tensors of 2nd order (i.e., fitted with 2 labels) are present in terms of generators g and in terms of a metric. By the vector calculus, g is representing a matrix while v and w are vectors. "**Measuring**" some state z means the special case y = tz with the measuring value t as some scalar, i.e., as a mere number. In this case, the label pair (a,b) is diagonal: b=a. Hence a measurement is given by

$$T\vec{z} = t\vec{z}, \quad t = T_a^b \text{ with } b=a.$$

More generally, a transformation T usually is represented by an exponential expression whose exponent splits off the imaginary unit together with some angle t as its current parameter as factors:

$$\mathbf{T = e^{-itg}} = \exp[-i\tfrac{t}{t'}(g'{\cdot}t')].$$

The true heart g of the transformation is its **generator**. In a quantised system, we are inclined to express the current angle t in terms of a "number of quanta" and to refer it to that number t' which would result in an equal distribution on the entire periphery of the circle.

Macroscopically, that quotient t/t', then, will usually become extremely small – functional theorists would call it infinitesimal. Squares and higher powers of t in the exponent will hence become negligible and may be cancelled. In fact, its "expansion according to Taylor" will end after its linear term, already:

$$\mathbf{T = e^{-itg} = 1 - itg + } \times$$

In physics, this linear approximation is a **metric**. In General Relativity, this "it" is proportional to the (tiny) gravitational constant.

With n dimensions, there are nxn transition modes, and the $T_a{}^b$ are components of an nxn-matrix. All n *diagonal* elements of the matrix are measurable independently of each other; they are "commensurable". If, in a superposition of such products vw, their labels run from 1 to n independently of each other, then, in this special case of 2 oppositely variant basic vectors, its components, by T–1 implicitly, are just representing a set of nxn generators g.

Let us collectively multiply m of these generators in a way that, in such a product, the upper label of one of the generators coincides with the lower label of the generator at its right-hand side. (The generator on its extreme left-hand side, here, will be used cyclically as the generator neighbouring the extreme right-hand one.) By summing over equal label pairs, we obtain **invariants**. Mathematicians also call them **Casimir operators of step m**:

$$C^{(1)} \equiv g_a{}^a,$$
$$\mathbf{C^{(2)} \equiv g_a{}^b g_b{}^a},$$
$$C^{(3)} \equiv g_a{}^b g_b{}^c g_c{}^a,$$
$$C^{(4)} \equiv g_a{}^b g_b{}^c g_c{}^d g_d{}^a, \text{ etc.}$$

(Einstein's summing convention: Pairs of equal labels have to be summed.)

The 1st-order Casimir, i.e., the sum of all diagonal elements of the matrix, is called the trace of the g. With just one vector v that satisfies w=v, v is the scalar square of the n-vector v according to the vector calculus. When returning to the original (v,w) pairs constituting the 2nd-order Casimir, the cancellation of their vw summation (not that over a and b, but that of the vectors v and w) together with resorting the components in one of the factors, we obtain the scalar product of w with v of the vector calculus, mediated by the metric g = (i/t) x log[T–1]:

$$\vec{w} \cdot \vec{v} = \Sigma_{a,b} \, (w^b \, (g_b{}^a \, v_a)).$$

In this case, g is taking over the role of a **metric**.

(By neglecting the leading unit matrix 1, sometimes, the complete metric ig will be limited to its linear Taylor term of the expansion of the transformation (T-1)/t, as well. For Einstein's GRT, t is a matrix, as well, essentially containing the gravitational constant and the masses involved. In QG, however, t is no matter of constants but really variable!)

With w=v and appropriate restrictions on the superposition structure of g, the above (invariant) right-hand side, when set equal to a constant, is representing the locus of the tips of vectors v on the **surface of an ellipsoid**.

(Observe that, independently of the above metric, people usually designate the distribution of imaginary factors, giving −1 in pairs, as the "metric" of the dynamic channel opposed to that of the connecting unit matrix in the reaction channel. Do not allow that ambiguity in defining a metric to give rise to confusion!)

7. Macrocosm vs. Microcosm

Now, by listening to quantum mechanics, we all are familiar with the case that there are components of classical vectors that in quantum mechanics are not commeasurable simultaneously any more. The traditionally quoted example is the 3-vector of spin, whose components on the x- and y-axes are not unique any longer, provided somebody has measured its value on its z-axis before. Classically, however, in the macrocosm, all 3 components still <u>are</u> measurable simultaneously.

What happened there? Well, particle physics knows 2 different ways of defining a variable. One of them is to define it as a component of representation space (Schrödinger's view), the other one is it to define it as an operator *acting* on representation space (Heisenberg's view). With a (fundamental) representation space of n dimensions, the operator will have a dimension equal to nxn. By an appropriate normalisation, the n dimensions of representation space can be identified on the diagonal of the nxn-dimensional operator space.

The latter dimensions represent the commeasurable components of (linear) variables (like $spin_0$ and $spin_3$). The remaining $nxn-n = n(n-1)$ components ($spin_1$ and $spin_2$), then, are the components that are no longer commeasurable. Hence, as a vector, spin only knows 2 directions (spin-up = $Spin_0$ plus $_3$, and spin-down = $_0$ minus $_3$); only as an operator, it is supplementing additional ones ($_1$ and $_2$)!

In the sense of vector calculus, the 1st-order Casimir represents the **microscopic scalar product** of two vectors in n dimensions; its 2nd-order Casimir represents their **macroscopic scalar product** in nxn dimensions. The non-diagonal components (a not equal to b), after its n diagonal components have been measured, i.e., been fixed, then just represent the, then, **non-commensurable** terms. According to the method of applying the law of (sufficiently) large numbers described in 1 dimension, now, in an approximative way, all directions of the macrocosm will be reproducible simultaneously.

This is the formal **transition from microscopic eigenvalues towards macroscopic expectation values** in the sense of New Physics: Tensor components that are non-commensurable in the microcosm (and spin or a vector is a special tensor) well might become commeasurable in the macrocosm! The macroscopic ellipsoid of the last chapter is the final result.

Thus, our concrete conclusion is: The space we are living in is not really 3-dimensional; **2 of our spatial directions are a macroscopic fake**! As components in 2-dimensional *spin space*, $spin_1$ and $spin_2$ are just sum and (i times) difference of spin-up and spin-down, respectively. Thus, they are redundant to $spin_0$ (sum in the singlet) and $spin_3$ (difference in the triplet). Only in *generator space*, all $2x2 = 4$ components (singlet and triplet) take over their own, independent place (as matrix elements), and a macroscopic superposition technique will make the non-diagonal elements accessible for a measurement.

Irreducibility, then, is nothing other than a formalism in order to state:

sum of products $\neq$ product of sums.

All these statements, first of all, relate to the reaction channel. In the dynamic channel, the fact remains that some of its dimensions, in addition, are multiplied by the imaginary unit – independently of whether the corresponding label is covariant or contravariant *(without sign change between the imaginary units as factors between both sides)*!

Contrary to the situation in the reaction channel, in the dynamic channel, here, the Pythagorean sum of squares of vector components might become negative, as well. *(And this happens both in an orthogonal and in a unitary product.)* Hence, we have to distinguish between 3 types of vectors in the dynamic channel:

time-like : square > 0,
space-like: square < 0,
light-like : square = 0.

In the dynamic channel, the ellipsoid quoted above will transform to a hyperboloid (whose density of quanta will thin out in the amount necessary).

8. Dirac's Legacy

The fusion of **Dirac**'s 4-dimensional spinor with his corresponding antispinor give a total spinor in 8-dimensions, indeed! Let us start with Dirac's first 4-spinor. The 4x4 generators acting on it in Quantum Gravity generate the 16 measurable basic components of dynamics. With i = 1,2,3 and CMS = centre-of-mass system, they are in the dynamic channel:

L_0	:	particle number,
L_i	:	spin *(3 components)*,
M_0	:	heavy mass,
M_i	:	Lorentz booster *(3 components)*,
P_0	:	energy,
P_i	:	momentum *(3 components)*,
Q_0	:	*(CMS-)*time,
Q_i	:	space *(3 components, in the CMS)*.

In this dynamic channel, **particle number** is the 1st-order, i.e., the linear Casimir operator; it is commeasurable with all 16 generators quoted. The linear Casimir of the reaction channel is **energy**, instead.

In **particle physics**, those 16 generators are well-known to be represented by Dirac's 16 "**gamma-matrices**". Altogether, they build up the "**Dirac-algebra**", which generates that common "complex Lie algebra" mentioned already. In principle, therefore, Dirac could have constructed Quantum Gravity as early as the 1930s.

But Dirac applied only 4 of his 16 gamma-matrices in the equation named after him. The reason was that his objective was merely to satisfy the **Klein-Gordon equation** of particle physics, which had been formulated too short, as well, which, last but not least, means Einstein's **equivalence principle** "heavy mass = inertial mass".

It will remain Dirac's secret why, at those times, he contented himself with that abridged version reproducing Special Relativity only, instead of penetrating towards General Relativity in one fell swoop by applying all 16 gamma-matrices.

Now, in the microcosm we are used to working right at the base of a single, individual physical state. Unlike in Quantum Gravity, Einstein's 4 spacetime components are considered to be commeasurable in classical quantum physics. There, it does not matter if we start some distance into the x-direction and, then, continue another distance into the y-direction − or v.v. ("parallelogram of forces").

This commensurability, however, does not hold in Einstein's GR any more. There, his coordinates are assumed to be curvilinear. If, for a comparison, we start on earth from the Galápagos Islands at the equator first northbound till we reach the Hudson Bay and, there, turn to the east until reaching Norway or Sweden, the exchange of both partial routes will first lead us from the Galápagos Islands towards the east in front of Recife in Brazil and from there towards the north to Iceland: The final points of both partial routes, in spite of equal distances, hence, are not the same in the polar coordinates of earth!

Einstein entered a "**metric** tensor" in order generally to treat curvilinear coordinates by geometrical means. That metric tensor, however, has proven to be such a hard problem that, up to now, nobody has been able to offer a convincing solution for its quantisation. From the perspective of QG, this is not surprising; for, his metric is representing a macroscopic superposition of a great number of microscopic details − which are not even complete, in addition.

In QG, the metric simply follows from the non-linearity of the higher Casimirs. Inserted into the world formula, polynomials of generators are set equal to constant, there. For the *macro*cosm, this automatically yields a **curvilinear surface** to be the locus of macroscopically observable measuring values representing the generators.

The 2nd-order Casimir, thus, gives the hyperboloid already mentioned. Its negative signs for _time_-like observables in the dynamic channel are a result of the squared imaginary unit. [*The non-commensurability of those curvilinear coordinates result from the non-commutativity (AB not equal to BA) of its generators (A,B,...) written down as matrices; cf. our 2 ways (corresponding to A and B) starting from the Galápagos Islands.*]

The fusion of Dirac's two 4-dimensional spinors to a common spinor in 8 dimensions spontaneously also solves the problem of why the part of our **world** accessible to us consists predominantly **of matter**, with antimatter entering only in terms of negligible, small "impurities": (Baryonic) Matter is described by its upper 4 components carrying positive particle number. We will later return to its lower 4 components carrying negative particle number.

By mathematics, the above 16 generators may be represented in terms of 4x4-matrices 4 of which are simultaneously diagonalisable – L_0, L_3, P_0, and Q_3, e.g. (With P_0 and Q_3 1 component of energy-momentum and 1 component of spacetime are commeasurable with each other.) In other words: Every quantum is representing a "**piece of dynamics**".

Depending on their combination, the components of two quanta, then, are just the 16 basic components of the above table. Hence, every quantum will represent 1 component of energy-momentum and 1 component of spacetime, each. (CMS-)**Spacetime and energy-momentum are generated by our quanta! Without these quanta there will be neither spacetime nor energy-momentum!** And the same will hold for the remaining 8 parameters L_μ and M_μ.

In order to prevent confusion: In Chapter 30, we shall still face another quantum number, N, which usually is called "particle number" as well. For distinction, hence, let us call the one of the above table N'.

While the other N, as a U(4,4) generator, will distinguish the <u>complete</u> Dirac-spinor (N>0) from the <u>complete</u> anti-spinor (N<0), the above N' will represent the 4-dimensional U(2,2) subset of the linear Casimir operators. For clarification, the effects of both generators on Dirac's a- and b-spin will be shown side by side, opposed to the absolute number of quanta N":

	N	N'	N"
a^+	+	+	+
b^-	+	−	+
b^+	−	−	+
a^-	−	+	+

9. *For Specialists Only: Mathematical Supplement*

In Dirac's 4 standard dimensions, the 4x4 = 16 dynamical generators are represented by

$$G_{\mu\nu} \propto a^+\left(\sigma_\mu \otimes \sigma_\nu\right)a^- \quad \text{with}$$

$$a^+ \equiv (a^+{}_1, a^+{}_2), \quad a^- \equiv \begin{pmatrix} a^-{}_1 \\ a^-{}_2 \end{pmatrix}.$$

A specialisation of the second label yields

$$G_{\mu0} = +\frac{1}{2}\left(a_1{}^+\sigma_\mu a_1{}^- + a_2{}^+\sigma_\mu a_2{}^-\right),$$

$$G_{\mu1} = +\frac{1}{2}\left(a_2{}^+\sigma_\mu a_1{}^- + a_1{}^+\sigma_\mu a_2{}^-\right),$$

$$G_{\mu2} = -\frac{i}{2}\left(a_2{}^+\sigma_\mu a_1{}^- - a_1{}^+\sigma_\mu a_2{}^-\right),$$

$$G_{\mu3} = +\frac{1}{2}\left(a_1{}^+\sigma_\mu a_1{}^- - a_2{}^+\sigma_\mu a_2{}^-\right),$$

Now, Dirac transcribed

$$a^\pm{}_m \equiv + \quad (a_1{}^\pm)_m \ ,$$

$$b^\mp{}_m \equiv +i(\sigma_1 a_2{}^\pm)_{m+2}$$

This, finally, gives rise to

$$G_{\mu0} = +\frac{1}{2}\left(a^+\sigma_\mu a^- - b^-\sigma_\mu b^+\right),$$

$$G_{\mu1} = -\frac{i}{2}\left(b^-\sigma_\mu a^- + a^+\sigma_\mu b^+\right),$$

$$G_{\mu2} = -\frac{1}{2}\left(b^-\sigma_\mu a^- - a^+\sigma_\mu b^+\right),$$

$$G_{\mu3} = +\frac{1}{2}\left(a^+\sigma_\mu a^- + b^-\sigma_\mu b^+\right).$$

With the labels 0 and i = 1,2,3, then, QG defines its 16 generators by

L_0	$\equiv G_{00}$,	L_i	$\equiv G_{i0}$,
P_0	$\equiv G_{03}$,	P_i	$\equiv G_{i1}$,
M_0	$\equiv G_{02}$,	M_i	$\equiv G_{i2}$,
Q_0	$\equiv G_{01}$,	Q_i	$\equiv G_{i3}$.

Those 6 Lorentz generators of Special Relativity embedded are highlighted in yellow.

Contrary to the situation in classical quantum field theories, QG is applying ordinary commutators (i.e., no "anticommutators"). Pauli's exclusion principle for fermions will be generated by the shell model (cf. Chapter 38).

*The „**commutators"** (commutation rules) of the U(2,2) generators (beyond those of the Lorentz group) are explicitly quoted, here:*

$$[P'_\mu, P'_\nu] = +i(\varepsilon_{\mu\nu\lambda} L_\mu + \delta_{\mu0} M_\nu - \delta_{0\nu} M_\mu)$$
$$[Q'_\mu, Q'_\nu] = -i(\varepsilon_{\mu\nu\lambda} L_\mu + \delta_{\mu0} M_\nu - \delta_{0\nu} M_\mu)$$
$$\textcolor{red}{[P'_\mu, Q'_\nu] = +i\,(-1)^{\delta_{\mu0}}\, \delta_{\mu\nu}\, M_0}$$
$$[M_0, P'_\mu] = +i\, Q'_\mu$$
$$[M_0, Q'_\mu] = +i\, P'_\mu$$

*After division by heavy mass (cf. Chapter 15), the red line represents the **canonical quantisation** of classical quantum theories. All additional lines together with it, then, are reproducing the **metric** of Quantum Gravity (QG). (By feeding the generators into the Casimirs and the Casimirs into the world formula, we observe that the metric is resulting in a curvilinear way; Einstein, once, had tediously done it in an incomplete way before by means of his General Relativity.)*

10. Cosmology and Particle Physics

In Dirac's 4 dimensions, our 2nd-order world formula (constant left-hand side) assumes the following form:

$$C_{SU(2,2)}^{(2)} \equiv + \left(P_0{}^2 - \vec{P}{}^2 - M_0{}^2 \right) - \left(Q_0{}^2 - \vec{Q}{}^2 \right) - \left(\vec{M}{}^2 - \vec{L}{}^2 \right).$$

In cosmology its first 5 dimensions (in red) here represent **Einstein's equivalence principle**; in particle physics (as an operator applied to some wave function), the **Klein-Gordon equation**. The central 4 terms (in blue) are CMS-spacetime, and the rightmost 6 parameters (in pink) represent the (2nd-order) Lorentz Casimir of Special Relativity (SRT).

In Special Relativity (SRT), all 3 parentheses are constant individually; in General Relativity (GRT) and in Quantum Gravity (QG), there are additional compensations among those individual parentheses. Einstein identified the origin of those deviations of GRT from SRT as "**geometrical forces**" triggered by the effect of **gravity**.

By Einstein's equivalence principle, the red parenthesis will vanish. In this case, those that remain will give distance Q_i (in blue) as a function of the Lorentz frame M_i (in pink). This is **Hubble's law**. All the rest beyond the equivalence principle yields a term

$$\lambda \equiv \left(Q_0{}^2 - \vec{Q}{}^2 \right) + \left(\vec{M}{}^2 - \vec{L}{}^2 + C_{SU(2,2)}^{(2)} \right).$$

Without knowing the content of its right-hand side, Einstein had already defined that remainder as his **cosmological constant**:

$$\left(P_0{}^2 - \vec{P}{}^2 \right) - M_0{}^2 - \lambda = 0.$$

The grey equation demonstrates that its content is by no means "constant" – equally, by the way, as the Hubble constant absorbed there.

When applied to particle physics, a non-vanishing cosmological constant, there, just is designating a **"virtual" state**:

$$\lambda \psi = \left(P_0{}^2 - \vec{P}^2 - M_0{}^2 \right) \psi \equiv \psi^{\text{virtual}}.$$

Feynman called its inverse expression (below in white) a "**propagator**". Solved for the wave function, this is

$$\psi = \frac{1}{\left(P_0{}^2 - \vec{P}^2 - M_0{}^2 \right)} \psi^{\text{virtual}}.$$

(In particle physics, those „internal" contributions of the "chiral forces" such as electromagnetism, e.g., still add to the cosmological constant. We are still getting to know them, later on. Because we do not actually know any universe beyond our own, there is no substance for considering additional respective parallels.) Anyway, for a stable particle we have the Klein-Gordon equation (parenthesis = 0). For energy-momentum = heavy mass, the propagator will become infinite, i.e., there is a **singularity**.

11. The Cosmic Hyperboloid

Solved for location as a function of time, the 2nd-order world formula of dynamics will read:

$$\overrightarrow{Q}^2 + Q_9^2 = r^2 + Q_0^2$$

with $\quad Q_9^2 = \left(P_0^2 - \overrightarrow{P}^2 - M_0^2\right) - \left(\overrightarrow{M}^2 - \overrightarrow{L}^2\right)$ and $\quad r^2 = C_{SU(2,2)}^{(2)}$.

For r and Q_9 as r-numbers, the yellow line represents the surface of some 1-shelled elliptic hyperboloid. Let us call it our **cosmic hyperboloid** (waist radius = r bar.):

$r^2 \geq 0, \quad Q_9^2 \geq 0$:

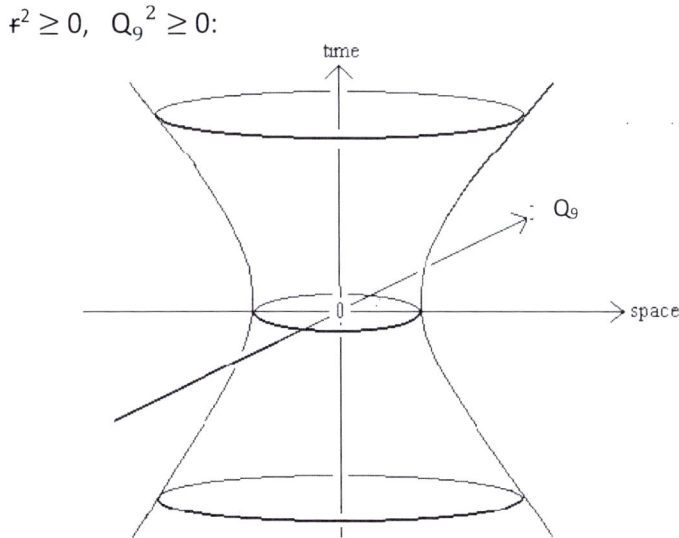

1. This hyperboloid is a set of macroscopic representations asymptotically thinning out, cut off somewhere in order to stay finite (cf. previous chapters);
2. For X_9=0, it asymptotically converges towards the "light cone" (space/time = constant, normalised to the velocity of light) from its *out*side;
3. It does *not* include the origin of our universe;

4. Asymptotically it shows up a **cosmic expansion** of space (into both time directions). (Waist radius = r.)

Point 2 describes **dark energy**: A particle at rest at time=0 (i.e., trajectory upwards) by increasing time will accelerate more and more outwards; for $X_9=0$, its velocity will asymptotically converge towards the velocity of light.

For an elementary particle described by the same world formula, its gradual thinning-out mode and its cut-off parameter (point 1) is a measure for its **particle radius**. For its explicit calculation, however, we would need the extended version of our QG by the octet containing the non-dynamical **"internal parameters"** (electric charge, isospin, ...) of the **"General Unified Theory (GUT)"** to the **"Theory of Everything (ToE)"**. QG is its "internal" singlet (cf. Chapter 24).

In the sketch above, the vertical plane $Q_9=0$ has been chosen as its conic section. When shifting that cut somewhat towards positive Q_9-values behind our actual drawing plane, the two branches of the hyperbola will approach each other, until, finally, both branches are touching each other at space=0 in the distance of the waist radius on the X_9-axis. The (correspondingly lower-dimensional) conic section will then degenerate to a double cone whose tips are touching each other, there. If we push that conic section still further behind the drawing plane, it will split again (see Chapter 12).

The double cone describes the situation we meet in the state where no forces are acting: Particles are moving with the constant velocity of light; all particles, *there*, have a **vanishing rest mass**. But that conic section might also be lying somewhat rotated about the time axis. In that case, particles are moving less fast: they are **massive**. In this case, particles would *not* anymore be accelerated to the speed of light; this points to another shortcoming of General Relativity. We shall identify it as shear forces and correct it (Chapter 29).

For an r-number Q_9 but imaginary r, the yellow line above represents a 2-shelled elliptic hyperboloid asymptotically approaching the double cone by superluminal velocity. The physical interpretation of such a case will be subject to a detailed discussion starting with Chapter 20.

In this representation, our cosmic hyperboloid's origin of time shows a minimal extension (of that part of) our universe observed by us. For optical surveying by means of the photon spectrum, however, opaqueness limits are present because of the ionisation of matter at high temperatures.

What happens behind that border is not observable by our actual technical state of the art. Conservative models assume some big-bang scenario – without, however, being able to explain those violations of physical conservation rules at the big-bang point accompanied by such an interpretation. With its cosmic hyperboloid, however, QG assumes some fluent transition of (our part of) the universe from a reflected (part of a) universe where time is running backwards; conservation rules, then, continue to hold true.

Another strong hint in favour of QG is its correct description of dark energy. In classical cosmology, there is no consistent explanation. Those fundamental, additional implications for cosmology (gravity) and particle physics (repulsion and attraction) resulting from this model continue to draw a consistent picture of this QG.

In pop science, cosmic expansion usually is compared with an inflating balloon: All points on its surface are equally moving away from each other, but none of them is central. The centre is located inside the balloon; however, it does not belong to our world, whose physics is playing on the surface. Nevertheless, the curvature radius is pointing into some additional direction perpendicular to it.

Einstein proudly emphasises that he eliminated that additional direction by the non-commutativity of his General Relativity. By doing so, however, he accumulated an unnecessary complication of his model. QG does not join that cat-and-mouse game. It accepts a priori that physics embraces more than those classical 4 spacetime dimensions (cf. Chapters 8, 9, 14, 19).

Physics will proceed on the surface of this hyperboloid. Einstein formulated his General Relativity in a differential-geometric way. His motion proceeded on geodetic lines. When, for QG, picking out some starting point and some starting direction on our cosmic hyperboloid, then, without additional forces, onward motion will follow the line of least curvature on the hyperboloid.

The starting direction will be given by some special linear combination of the generators. The directions (kept constant) perpendicular to the direction of motion define some hypersurface which, with this number of macroscopic dimensions, will represent some different hyperboloid one dimension less. Its cutting surface with our cosmic hyperboloid just is the **geodetic line** we had been looking for.

In the presence of chiral forces (electromagnetism, etc.) from the GUT, the world formula will be extended by corresponding supplementary terms. The geodetic line then generated in the correspondingly higher-dimensional cosmic hyperboloid will have some higher dimension, as well. Its construction principle, however, is identical.

Points exterior to our cosmic hyperboloid will belong to different values of its Casimirs. If you like, they are located in different, parallel universes.

12. Cosmic Inflation

Provided Q_9 is big enough, the conic section through our cosmic hyperboloid, when keeping Q_9 constant, will yield a 2-shelled elliptic hyperboloid approaching the related lower-dimensional Q_9-light cone from its interior:

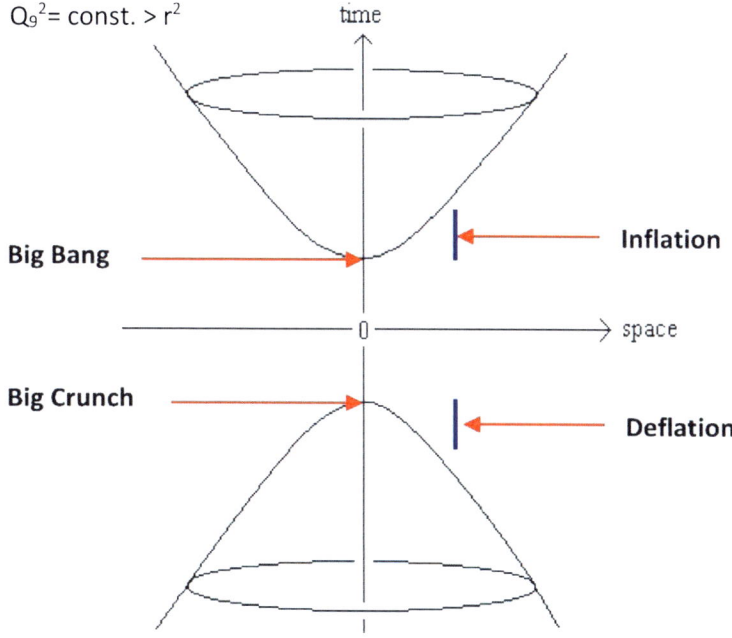

Its upper shell is bounded downwards. That means that the upper shell of the selected Q_9-slice has a definite starting point of time called a "**big bang**". *Immediately* before, there is "nothing" (within this slice) – the opposite, lower shell is far away. The tangent plane annexed to that point is horizontal. That means that the temporal space-expansion rate of the upper shell will formally be infinite at its start and will then gradually slow down. In literature, this behaviour is called "**cosmic inflation**".

On the lower shell, everything is inverted: With increasing (negative) time, space will be ending up in a **deflation**ary collapse called a "**big crunch**".

Observe, however, that all that is playing on a restricted *conic section*: But physics will be following the *full* QG embracing all those conic sections: A particular section might express some special, approximated behaviour, at most.

Cosmic inflation is controversially debated in the literature. For, its only experimental hint – if there is one – is an almost even, isotropic long-scale distribution of galaxies in our universe. Cosmic inflation was originally invented to explain it. The official opinion is that structure should have developed regularly, starting from some distribution present shortly after the big bang, when the mutual interactions had become weak enough not any more to derange the distribution achieved too much.

Hence, that even, isotropic distribution we observe should actually be the smoothing result frozen in of those equalising strong mutual interactions of a time when our universe was small enough. In order to freeze in that situation, there should have occurred a phase of "fast" expansion. This would be cosmic inflation. On the cosmic hyperboloid of the preceding chapter, this would address that phase after its strongest curvature about time=0 but before its transition into the asymptotic region. Do not be troubled by the apparent contradiction between the two representations of our cosmic hyperboloid to approach the light cone behaviour from its *outside* and of cosmic inflation approaching it from *inside*: The two sketches are dealing with different numbers of dimensions!

In order to obtain the double-shelled structure of cosmic inflation, Q_9 must become greater than the waist radius. Provided we started right "upwards" at time=0, this would mean that our originally radial motion within the (space, Q_9)-plane would have to change its direction by 90° within this (space, Q_9)-plane when entering the conic section lying perpendicular to the radial direction! Even without a particular calculation, thus, it looks questionable if nature – by a classical interpretation of physical laws – would engage in such an escapade, indeed.

Quite apart from the fact that motion of real particles by a super-luminal velocity would contradict all physical experience! Classical physics, hence, recommends that we distinguish between an **absolute motion** and a **motion relative** to a spacetime limited by its expanding surface. Absolute, here, has the significance of being relative to all 15 dimensions of the world formula, and relative means relative to the, then, just 14 dimensions of the expanding surface left perpendicular to the related curvature radius.

The latter opinion agrees with the doctrine supported by the Einstein faction of cosmology, according to which the "physical" velocity is added to the related local expansion velocity to give rise to the total, absolute velocity. When thinking that idea right to the end, however, we arrive at something like a(n immaterial) supporting ether structure – a model Einstein, in fact, long since had eliminated from physics by his relativity theories. Only without such a **supporting structure** can the laws of physics (like causality, e.g.) be true again.

This leads to a clear statement: With its convergence towards zero, the time difference in the denominator of velocity is the trigger of an unphysical singularity in the conic section. Hence, necessarily there should still be present some additional parameter – something like a **2nd type of time** adding to ordinary time – to yield a sufficiently great total value (in the denominator).

A first hint was already given by Feynman when he introduced **virtual masses** into physics (which violate Einstein's equivalence principle). By our model of black-hole physics (starting with Chapter

20), we learn that heavy mass will quite easily take over this role in QG, indeed. For, contrary to classical physics, heavy mass, here, is variable – only to an essentially much more "rigid" extent than ordinary time! (This, however, is a matter of the system of units, cf. Chapter 28.)

Conclusion:
Cosmic inflation is based on the same misleading classical misinterpretation of incomplete data collection as the singularity behind the event horizon of a black hole. Cosmologists systematically ignore the point, which has its source in the reduction of dimensions in the transition from our cosmic hyperboloid to cosmic inflation:

By an inadequate interpretation, such a **cut-down of dimensions** definitely might lead to the problem that a consistent representation with subluminal velocities (cosmic hyperboloid) will degenerate to an unphysical representation containing superluminal velocities! In the given case, this is the variability of heavy masses in extreme situations swept under the table by this restriction – whether on a small scale (Feynman's virtual masses) or on a large scale (event horizon, etc.).

13. The Matryoshka Principle

That alternative claim of Quantum Gravity that it can describe our cosmos and the world of quanta by the same procedure looks more interesting. Its concept is as speculative as saying that our universe should be just one of many joining the ping-pong game that universes are playing with each other in order to build up larger clusters of universes – similarly to the behaviour of individual quanta building up an elementary particle.

Only those minor disturbances acting back on *our* universe by its external *interactions* would trigger the creation of those major compounds observed by astronomers instead of keeping their otherwise homogeneous distribution of matter. In an analogy with those inelastic scattering results of elementary particles, our universe would then have to be understood as a result of colliding or decaying precursor universes.

That analogy would not be universe-particle nor particle-quantum but directly universe-quantum. Particles, molecules, crystals, etc., would just denote intermediate structures, like plasma continuing to develop towards stars, galaxies, and astronomical clusters at higher temperatures.

A universe, then, would not be created as the result (by the dynamic channel) of some temporally developing "big bang" acting like a lonely "grain of seed" but as an entire unit, at all places and times simultaneously, independently of time (by the reaction channel). Only this way will lead towards Bell's superdeterminism. Compare it with the behaviour of individual stars (corresponding to quanta) when galaxies (corresponding to particles) are colliding – except that galaxies are no "irreducible" representations.

We would expect a universe (*free* of external interactions) to be "irreducible" in the mathematical sense of group theory. Then, however, elementary particles in its interior could not be "irreducible" *as well*!

For, it just is the queer definition of irreducibility that it does not admit any decomposition into further irreducible blocks. Hence, an elementary particle will have to be understood as some constructive superposition knot of a multitude of neighbouring components of the universe! Such a "knot", however, also will mean a limited extension and a **limited lifetime** ("death").

Thus, on the level of a simple elementary particle, already, statistics grossly interferes. It is the base of the non-valence part of a particle. Traditional particle physicists usually add it in terms of continuous arguments to their otherwise discrete spinors – not really knowing where they have their origin.

But let us return to our universe/quantum hierarchy. The base of QG has been laid down by human principles: Dynamics is some biological construct; the reaction channel is original. A transition towards differing orders of magnitude does not change the principles. That ping-pong game of universes could take place within some kind of *super*-universe by whose view *our* universes represent nothing else than constructive interferences of its components.

Corresponding decompositions, then, should exist there, too. Simply from the human view, all that taken together would correspond to some nesting of structures following the principle of Russian matryoshka dolls. This interpretation of a unit representing some lower hierarchy as merely some superposition of components of the next higher hierarchy – as group theory imposes it on us – would permit us even to pass their borderlines: This would admit a travel sailing across them – there is no evidence for an *absolute* borderline to exist in physics.

14. Dimensions

In quantum physics, we again and again observe that the reaction channel is primary. Nevertheless, classical statements, at most, refer to the dynamic channel. The reason is that standard experiments are often executed more easily by reactions setting a state at rest into motion than by "inelastic" reactions changing its composition. Hence, let us follow that trend.

Half of Dirac's 16 generators of the dynamic channel are 4x4-matrices made of r-numbers, the other half of purely imaginary numbers. After taking off their linear Casimir operator L_0, let me reorder the remaining 15 generators according to the following 6x6-scheme:

SU(2,2):

0	$-P'_0$	$-M_0$	$-P'_3$	$-P'_2$	$-P'_1$
$+P'_0$	0	$+Q'_0$	$-M_3$	$-M_2$	$-M_1$
$+M_0$	$-Q'_0$	0	$-Q'_3$	$-Q'_2$	$-Q'_1$
$+P'_3$	$+M_3$	$+Q'_3$	0	$+L_1$	$-L_2$
$+P'_2$	$+M_2$	$+Q'_2$	$-L_1$	0	$+L_3$
$+P'_1$	$+M_1$	$+Q'_1$	$+L_2$	$-L_3$	0

The upper right-hand half of those generators, quoted in Chapter 8 above, are here reflected with opposite signs to the lower left-hand side of the scheme. The current denotation "**SU(2,2)**" is its mathematical abbreviation telling us that 2 of their 4 dimensions are time-like and the remaining 2 dimensions space-like.

The "S" stands for "special", i.e., the linear Casimir is taken off, and the "U" stands for "unitary", i.e., these generators would conserve probability – *provided all of them would either be all time-like or all space-like.* Due to their mixture of time- with space-like properties, the corresponding transformation group generated by these entries is called a "special **pseudo-unitary** group in 2 time-like plus 2 space-like dimensions".

Let me rename these generators without changing their positions in the above scheme. The result is a scheme whose generators are "skew-symmetric" with respect to their label pairs ($L_{ij} = -L_{ji}$):

SO(2,4):

0	$+L_{65}$	$+L_{64}$	$+L_{63}$	$+L_{62}$	$+L_{61}$
$+L_{56}$	0	$+L_{54}$	$+L_{53}$	$+L_{52}$	$+L_{51}$
$+L_{46}$	$+L_{45}$	0	$+L_{43}$	$+L_{42}$	$+L_{41}$
$+L_{36}$	$+L_{35}$	$+L_{34}$	0	$+L_{32}$	$+L_{31}$
$+L_{26}$	$+L_{25}$	$+L_{24}$	$+L_{23}$	0	$+L_{21}$
$+L_{16}$	$+L_{15}$	$+L_{14}$	$+L_{13}$	$+L_{12}$	0

The transformation group we thus obtain is a "special **pseudo-orthogonal** group in 2 time-like plus 4 space-like dimensions". An "orthogonal" group denotes a rotation group. This SO(2,4) is also known as the "**conformal group**".

Thus Dirac's 4 pseudo-unitary dimensions are equivalent to 6 pseudo-orthogonal dimensions. Einstein's 4 dimensions 0,1,2,3 are labelled here as 5,1,2,3. The 3 generators solely labelled by pairs out of 1,2,3, here, are *spin*; Einstein did not apply spin! And the dimensions 4 and 6 were unknown to him. In other words, he used them as being constant, not varying.

Einstein's equations refer to *macroscopic* situations. His (continuous) description by differential geometry can be considered as a (defective) **projection of those 6 dimensions** with the dimensions 4 and 6 kept constant. In Einstein's "old" denotation we find:

$$(1,4) = 1_{\text{old space}},$$
$$(2,4) = 2_{\text{old space}},$$
$$(3,4) = 3_{\text{old space}};$$
$$(5,4) = 0_{\text{old time}}.$$

Correspondingly, energy-momentum will become

$$(1,6) = 1_{\text{old momentum}},$$
$$(2,6) = 2_{\text{old momentum}},$$
$$(3,6) = 3_{\text{old momentum}};$$
$$(5,6) = 0_{\text{old energy}}.$$

While Einstein still used spacetime in an exclusively geometrical formulation (by Ricci's curvature tensor), he left energy-momentum (in terms of his stress-energy tensor) vaguely open, depending on the special problem to be treated. By applying its world formula, QG explicitly breaks down _all_ those generators to their irreducible conformal roots.

In Einstein's projection, heavy mass, L_{46}, will become a constant, as well. This prevented him from noticing that _heavy mass_ could become "**virtual**" as shown by **Feynman** when applying Dirac's formalism. (A "virtual" mass deviates from the rest mass as measured experimentally. A _"virtual particle"_, defined by carrying a virtual heavy mass, is unstable.) In QG, a virtual state will belong to the same representation its stable state does (if existing) because mass is not invariant.

Quantum _Mechanics_ usually keeps heavy mass (4,6) and the Lorentz frame (3,5) in spin direction (1,2) diagonal. Now, QG knows **2 directions** to be **time-like**. In relativity, there is just 1 time-like direction. As elaborated above, with its just 1 time axis, the variational principle, based on the Lagrangian formalism, is thus not an appropriate means for treating fundamental physics.

QG is based on the set of its quanta. Its structure is the result of expanding this set in terms of group theory. Space and time are just 4 of its 16 generators. When defining "**background-independence**" as the property that its spacetime metric is a solution of dynamics, then QG is background-independent, as well – like General Relativity.

15. The Technical Base of Philosophy

Why do we distinguish between time and space? That imaginary factor multiplying the time-like dimensions in the dynamic channel – where does it come from?

The reaction channel, we learned, is the answer to probability conservation, which, for n dimensions, needs strictly "unitary" representations of the type U(n) (or subgroups, respectively). In 8 dimensions, this is a U(8). Due to 8 = 2**3, its fundamental spinor in 8 dimensions allows for construction by a 3-fold nesting of 2-dimensional U(2)-spinors, each:

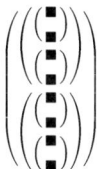

For their 2x2=4 generators applied to such a U(2)-spinor, just the **4 Pauli matrices** are appropriate, which, up to a factor 1/2, are giving its half-integral spin values. With the exception of Pauli's matrix # 2, which is imaginary, their elements consist of r-numbers.

Now, classical physics (before Planck) predominantly work with r-numbers, however. In order to stay with r-numbers, one way out could have been always to double the spin components, thus giving (topologically "double-connected") pair products. Their two half-integral spins would thus add up to integer spins.

At least, this has been the traditional trick. For, people are used to lumping spin and orbital angular momentum together, although both notions have nothing in common: Spin is a tensor operator of 2nd order, and orbital angular momentum one of 4th order! According to this misleading way of speaking, "classical physics" is said not to have known half-integral spins. This, of course, is nonsense: Classical physics did not know any spin at all: spin was only detected in 1926!

As asked for, all (pair) generators would stay real by this topological trick – however, all spins would result as integers. Provided we want to maintain the (topologically "single-connected") standard, then we have to multiply Pauli's 2nd matrix by the imaginary unit, instead. Then, however, the result will become a pseudo-unitary U(1,1) replacing the unitary U(2), and those olden topological antics will become dispensable.

Dirac's additive split of the 8 dimensions of Quantum Gravity into 2 spinors of 4 dimensions each (one for a quantum, and another one for its antiquantum) will correspondingly also split its 8x8-dimensional metric into 2x2 sections of (8/2)x(8/2) dimensions, each. The rupture between Dirac's quanta and his antiquanta showing up in the dynamic channel propagates in terms of the **event horizon** to cosmology.

For the metric, this split of the 8-dimensional representation space into 2 separate sections of 4 dimensions, each, means a split into 2x2 = 4 sections. Besides its rupture with respect to the event horizon, there will be another rupture in the metric with respect to what I called the "**Lorentz horizon**" in my Chapter 19. In cosmology, it separates the domain "after the big bang" from that "**before the big bang**".

For Einstein, just <u>one</u> of these domains was present. Due to his concept of ignoring irreducibility in his representations, his components after the big bang overlap those before the big bang. Due to the additional incompleteness of his representations, their defective extrapolations towards the additional 3 domains inevitably produced mathematical **inconsistencies** showing up in terms of singularities, e.g. Quantum Gravity, by construction, is free of such singularities.

The transition among the 4 domains proceeds by means of the parity operators C of **charge conjugation** and T of **time reversal** (cf. Chapter 19). By experiment, the transition over the event horizon by applying charge conjugation C proved to be the most rigid one (needing the maximal experimental effort).

This is the reason why Dirac had to position his rupture right between a particle and its antiparticle. Analogously, non-relativistic quantum mechanics had to allocate its 2-dimensional rupture right between Dirac's a- and b-spin because, experimentally, the resistance against a relativistic Lorentz boost is much stronger than against a non-relativistic rotation.

Mathematics went about implementing those ruptures by a sign change in its metric. The event horizon imposed the separation of a spinor from its antispinor on Dirac, and relativity the separation of his a-spin from b-spin. Altogether, this forced Quantum Gravity to split the 8 dimensions of its dynamic channel into the pair U(2,2) + U(2,2).

The above 3-fold nesting will now give some U(4,4). Correspondingly, Dirac's split into 2 spinors of 4 dimensions, each, will result in a pseudo-unitary U(2,2). Somehow – I am not a biologist – the latter effect must have propagated down through all **human evolution**. How else could we explain that we are observing the world we are living in by **pseudo-unitary dynamics**?

But our biological evolution goes still deeper: Why do we observe our environment by categories of space, time, and velocity at all? Even the old, mechanistic view of our world before Planck had already laid to rest that non-linear velocity by separating off the "**heavy-mass**" factor, whose nature, up to now, is officially understood just that little. The rest, then, is replaced by the more abstract, but *linear* momentum, while the interpretation of energy in all its variants of manifestation was still reserved to thermodynamics for a longer time.

Only Quantum Gravity, analogously, fell back on the ancient notion of a linear "**centre-of-mass** spacetime" in order, contrary to the master himself, to erase Einstein's classical, non-linear spacetime from basic physics.

Einstein's _non-linear_, classical spacetime X and velocity V result from their _linear_ CMS-types Q and P by:

$$P_\mu = M_0 \cdot V_\mu$$
$$Q_\mu = M_0 \cdot X_\mu$$

Here again, it is a matter of our evolution why we observe those quotients V and X in daily life – and not the original P and Q, instead. This time, the answer is more plausible, however: Nature has made us learn to "feel" the averaged, macroscopic world – the microscopic world is usually too fine for our senses, too much detailed. Now, "feeling" is a matter of consciousness and survival. And survival, that temporary, local existence of constructive superposition knots, is the fundamental key inevitably necessary to human consciousness as we know it!

Let me still add a hint to the expert: The above nesting of two 2-dimensional U(1,1)-spinors giving Dirac's spinor in 4 dimensions, then, has been resorted to by Dirac himself to give two U(2)-pairs that in his notation are called "**a-spin**" (black square + red round) and "**b-spin**" (black round + red square). Hence, his "**Spin**", conceptually, is a rather artificial construction giving rise to sophisticated sign problems:

$$\begin{pmatrix} \begin{pmatrix} \blacksquare \\ \color{red}\blacksquare \end{pmatrix} \\ \begin{pmatrix} \bullet \\ \color{red}\bullet \end{pmatrix} \end{pmatrix} \Rightarrow \begin{pmatrix} \begin{pmatrix} \blacksquare \\ \color{red}\bullet \end{pmatrix} \\ \begin{pmatrix} \bullet \\ \color{red}\blacksquare \end{pmatrix} \end{pmatrix}.$$

U(2)-components are rotated into each other by trigonometric functions (cos, sin) on the periphery of a circle. U(1,1)-components do so by their corresponding hyperbolic functions (cosh, sinh) on the two branches of a hyperbola. For sufficiently small rotation angles, you cannot distinguish if you are moving on a circle or on a branch of a hyperbola. Cosmologists, hence, should be careful when extrapolating distances at a longer scale: an exponential dilation or compression could be active! Special care will be needed if a velocity is measured not by dividing linear momentum by heavy mass but in terms of a differential quotient of the *non*-linear variants of space and time provided *both* of them are equally defined hyperbolically!

16. What Is Time, What Space?

A "reaction" is relating an **output** to an **input**. Input and output are members of 2 different classes. In the reaction channel, mathematicians calculate the probability of an output resulting from an input by projecting them onto each other. By using the output of one reaction to serve as the input for another one, reactions can be chained to give ordered sequences.

This intermediate identification of an input with a neighbouring output might be interpreted as the annihilation ("destruction") of that output followed by the "creation" of the new input. More generally, the pair combination of such a "**destruction operator**" with a "**creation operator**" (up to some normalisation factor) is called a "generator". In Quantum Gravity, this notion is broken down to its individual quanta. There, a "**generator**" is a **bilinear** combination of a pair of quanta belonging to 2 different classes: one output quant with one input quant.

Traditional physics does not distinguish between "quanta" and "quarks" (leptons included) as its fundamental constituents. Quarks (and leptons), however, consist of some multitude of quanta. Elementary particles quite generally – and quarks are elementary particles – arrange their quanta in terms of a **valence part** and a **non-valence part**, each. The valence part defines their "internal" parameters (electric charge, etc.) plus spin in terms of discrete labels, the **non-valence part** the rest of its *dynamic* parameters in terms of continuous "arguments". (The *Higgs* Model is some poor auxiliary tool for roughly simulating a few of the properties to be attributed to the non-valence part.)

By misinterpreting older experiments, the "Standard Model" of elementary particles culminates in the discretionary postulate demanding that quarks should occur either in triples only or coupled to quark-antiquark pairs. Meanwhile, this strange law of "3 quarks only" is experimentally disproved; but it is still deeply present in the brains.

For the construction of Quantum Gravity with its quanta replacing the quarks as its fundamental bricks, however, that categorical postulate has represented a centennial disaster! For, that old "law" combines 2 statements with each other: "3 quarks only" and "in terms of 3 quarks". That "only" part has been disproved. But that "in terms of 3" part still survives as "**quark confinement**" and, up to now, the official literature has not been able to substantiate that strange law theoretically. QG is the only model to derive it explicitly (by the topology of the "internal" forces).

Again, the fatal thoughtlessness shows up by which in modern times, since Schrödinger, Pauli, and Bohr, special experiments are hastily pushed into the position of generally mandatory laws without any compelling argument, thus promoting no favour to generations to come, whose creative power is cut that profoundly! No surprise that for a century up to now there has been no real progress in the official literature with respect to Einstein's world formula.

Einstein still developed his relativity theories in a top-down procedure; he still was well conscious of the scope of his policy. After World War II, however, particle physicists widely emigrated towards North America. There, the bottom-up method dominates. There, economic speeding is an asset. Results have to be published before competitors get their first chance to be noticed. American research lives for the moment. Sustainability means a luxury nobody really wants to afford. In such an environment, Einstein simply starved spiritually at Princeton.

This way, the Anglo-Saxon world is the origin of mixing up the destruction operators reserved for the output with the creation operators reserved for the input. Thus, particles are "created" from nothing and "destroyed" to nothing in pairs ("2nd quantisation", "vacuum polarisation"). The "**number of quanta**" loses its property of being a conserved quantity (of the 8-dimensional QG in its reaction channel). This means the unphysical transition of a discrete, finite-dimensional representation of QG towards its continuous, infinite-dimensional representation in favour of functional analysis.

This method of artificially introducing unnecessary infinities produced a jumble of singularities in particle physics. A remedy has been found in terms of a subsequent, global "renormalisation" having to debug the problems more by persuasion than by conviction. Perhaps, I did not yet mention distinctly enough that the above creation-destruction concept was originally developed within a probability setting, i.e., within a unitary surrounding. Within the dynamic channel, however, this concept technically works as well, but the destruction technique will not yield a **probability message** anymore!

Now, *Feynman's diagrams* describing particle reactions perpetually mix up actions belonging to the reaction channel with those ("propagators") belonging to the dynamic channel. In a correct handling, both channels would have to be properly separated from each other. Otherwise, those dynamic sections should be expanded in the "unitary" terms of the reaction channel in order to respect probability conservation each for itself. Literature knows examples where corresponding amplitudes are expanded in terms of "**form factors**". In QG, the "virtual states" needed are provided quite naturally by the world formula, already.

Let us, however, return to the starting problem: What are **space and time**? Like all generators, first of all, they are **bilinear** combinations of destruction operators with creation operators. But *microscopically just 1 of its 4 components is commeasurable* at a time. After "diagonalising" one of these spacetime operators, it will count its corresponding quanta. The result, then, is a **number of quanta** of the respective type ("diagonalised" before). But functional-analytic models just *drop* this "number of quanta" that important!

(Technical hint for the expert: Compare it with determining a spin component. Spacetime is <u>pseudo</u>-unitary, indeed; but in QG its representation is finite-dimensional. Hence, time allows for the <u>same</u> "diagonalisation" procedure as a space component. Compare the concept – sum vs. integral – with finite against infinite Fourier transformations.)

17. Enigmatic Time

According to Einstein's level of knowledge, nature is invariant against time reversal on its microscopic level. This statement contains two level restrictions. The microscopic restriction excludes thermodynamics and General Relativity; Einstein's restriction excludes the world formula, dark energy, dark matter, particle number, parities, and black holes.

On this rather limited realm, the above statement refers to (sections of) the dynamic Casimir operator of 2nd order, where time is contained in its squared form only. Here, of course, time is reversible, like space; the direction of the time arrow (towards the future or towards the past) does not matter. Particle experiments support this theoretical finding.

In daily life, however, time behaves differently from space: Time always proceeds ahead, never backwards. Cosmologists trace it back to **cosmic expansion**, where space increases with increasing time. And their conjecture is that more space means less **entropy**. The **arrow of time**, then, will simply be following decreasing entropy. *(Entropy is that property that a cup falling from the table will break to pieces at a rigid floor; the other way around, however, its pieces will never restore the cup and jump back onto the table.)*

3 essential problems are left:

1. Why does an increasing space give rise to a decreasing entropy?
2. Why is time so indecisive, first appearing reversible, the next moment irreversible? What makes the difference?
3. Why, then, does cosmic expansion not provide some **arrow of space**, as well?

First of all, the number of quantum pairs is irrelevant for entropy: Generators just *convert* such pairs (energy to CMS-space, e.g.), but they do not *add new* <u>states</u>.

Generators like space and time are bilinear expressions from 2 different classes. Their gross quantum numbers, however, can be reconstructed within one of those two classes, as well. In this case, the multiplication of such a pair of creation operators with a single creation operator will mean something like an extended form of "spin addition" (whatever this might mean to the layman).

Such an extended spin addition – mathematicians call it a "**reduction**" – will follow rules different from those used for applying a pure generator. A generator will simply *replace* 1 of the creation operators it is applied to by its own creation part; this is a 1:1 action. Thus, it just will mix up the components of one and the same representation of the other. The pathway giving the final point created by applying the generator to some starting point, hence, can be reversed uniquely: it is "**reversible**".

A "reduction", however, still will yield new, further representations that have not been considered before – no matter if they were present already or not. A reduction will thus yield *more than one* final point. Such a "forked pathway" cannot usually be reversed uniquely: it is "**irreversible**". For, the inverse way is forked as well!

This latter method is the standard one in our cosmos. In our hyperboloid it leads us from one of its microscopic time slices to the neighbouring one next door. It represents the source of "cosmic expansion". (Remember: The cosmic hyperboloid is a figure within the *dynamic* channel, and dynamics is "open", it is not subject to probability conservation!)

To make a long story short: Progression in time adds up both effects. On the microscopic level, a neighbouring time slice will not look much different, i.e., the reduction process will still be negligibly small: Time still looks reversible. With an increasing time difference, however, the new space quanta created by the reduction process of cosmic expansion will accumulate more and more. At some time, they will cease being negligible: From then on, time will appear irreversible to us.

The number of states, however, will not vary much; but the space available to them will enlarge: **entropy decreases**. The **time arrow**, hence, will point from the inside towards the outside direction of our universe. We **"feel" cosmic expansion** by the irreversible progression of time. Without cosmic expansion, time would stop running, our clocks would stop ticking! The transition between reversibility and irreversibility will be fluent, though.

The same procedure applies to space, as well – there will be an "**arrow of space**", too! Only, by the speed c of light,

$$1 \text{ sec} \approx c \cdot 10^{10} \text{ cm}.$$

By this large proportionality factor, we need some much longer distance before we are going to feel cosmic expansion by distance, as well. *Therefore*, space *still* looks reversible to us.

According to Quantum theory, the energy generator gives rise to the progression of time. *(This is a result of Schrödinger's Fourier transformation.)* In QG a change in CMS-time (5,4) by energy (5,6) will proceed at the expense of heavy mass (4,6), however: All 3 generators are coupled to an SU(1,1). Varying entropy, hence, will give rise to a varying mass value, as well! This is the consistency trap Einstein was not conscious of: His masses are invariant.

Heavy mass (4,6) is a time-like generator, too. Its mathematical behaviour is like that of CMS-time (4,5). In physics, however, "both times" have different normalisations (cf. Chapter 28). In QG, time is measured in units of c (speed of light), heavy mass in units of "q bar". The units differ by orders of magnitude. Heavy mass is by far more lethargic than CMS-time. It needs much higher relative energies in order to show its variability. Keywords: "virtual states", dark matter, event horizon.

18. Demystified Measuring Process

Rather daring rumours are spread with the measuring process. Thus, it is said to be responsible for a *"breakdown" of Schrödinger's wave equation*. The fact is that physics is confounded here with mathematics, and the **cooperation of the measuring device** is culpably ignored.

In general, a physical state to be measured will not necessarily happen to be "diagonal" a priori, already. It will represent some mixture of various states. First of all, a measurement will therefore have to "diagonalise" that state. But how does that happen physically?

By definition, a measuring device can transform an (irreducible) input arbitrarily accepted into some well-defined output, its "**measuring result**". To do so, a finite number of output channels will be disposable; the device will have to "decide" which one to use. For example, think of a pencil balancing on its tip. Such a state is unstable. The pencil will topple down in some direction.

On the macroscopic level, this direction will hardly be predictable; microscopically, however, the direction is a function of the internal structure of its molecules, of the cross wind, etc. Therefore, microscopically, some well-defined causal chain will proceed which, on the macroscopic level, can hardly be queried in a rush. Last but not least, something will proceed, there, which, on the macroscopic level, will be interpreted as some *rotation* of the input towards the output direction. More generally, our statement will be: The property of a measuring device is a "**unitary rotation**" of its input into one of its output directions.

But what does the official literature tell us? That a measuring process is "*projecting*" its input onto the output channel. Tacitly it keeps secret that such a "*projection*" is a singular operation, i.e., that it is violating probability conservation. On the other hand, it is exactly this violation which then, is denounced as "mysterious" and "not understood"!

19. Event Horizon

The 4 components of a Dirac-spinor transform according to Special Relativity by using the SO(2,4)-dimensions 5,1,2,3; its dimensions 4 and 6 are kept fixed. This, however, fixes the relative signs of time (4,5), energy (6,5), and heavy mass (4,6), as well. In order to change them, particle physicists invented 2 parities, T and C; their product is proportional to P:

- **T = time reversal** (time, here, is not CMS- but ordinary time),
- **C = charge conjugation,**
- **P = space inversion** (= ordinary **"parity"** in 3 directions).

(Beware of confounding parity P with energy-momentum P: In an alphabet, the number of its letters is limited!) Dirac once defined C to transform an incoming particle to an outgoing antiparticle (with implicit reversal of ordinary time). Thus, all 3 parities multiply their results by parity-specific sign factors. In addition, T, especially, switches the sign of ordinary time, and C the sign of heavy mass, in addition.

T and C, hence, divide their entire area of application into 2 sections, each – both together, hence into 4 sections, altogether. If we arrange them to deliver a 2x2-pattern, T will correspond to Pauli's matrix # 1, and C to Pauli's matrix # 2. If we do not define the inner-most nesting step of parity P in Chapter 15 by Pauli's matrix #3 but by #0, then their product will yield a term proportional to Pauli's matrix #3, whose squared form is the unity matrix. Their 3-fold product, then, just is the **TCP-theorem** known from particle physics:

$$TCP = -1.$$

The total application area, however, is not 2- but 8-dimensional, so its 4 sections are (8/2 =) 4-dimensional, each. If we chose the upper one of their application areas to be a Dirac-spinor of an SO(2,4), then, up to some reordering of components, the lower one will be its related antispinor of an SO(4,2).

Their corresponding pseudo-unitary groups, in both cases, however, are U(2,2) groups. In the latter case, the former 2 upper dimensions are exchanged with the former 2 lower dimensions. Now, the complete configuration group is a dynamic U(4,4). The U(2,2)-metric of its upper Dirac-spinor is $(+,+,-,-)$, that of its lower antispinor, hence, $(-,-,+,+)$. The cardinality (number of its discrete elements) is equal in both U(2,2)-subconfigurations.

Formally, the 2nd of both U(2,2) subgroups is derived from its 1st one by multiplying its generators with the imaginary unit. Charge conjugation C is here represented by some rotation about the (imaginary) heavy-mass axis in the (4,6)-plane, while time reversal T is represented by a corresponding rotation in the (4,5)-plane about the (imaginary) CMS-time axis.

Due to the imaginary rotation axes of time-like generators, C and T, like parity P, belong to the reaction channel, where they are quite ordinary transformations. In the dynamic channel, however, they manage the transition over the ruptures, which, in the case of charge conjugation C, is called an "**event horizon**" (bold red line); in the case of time reversal T (thin red line), let us baptize it the "**Lorentz horizon**":

U(2,2)	U(2,2)
particle no. > 0	particle no. < 0
$time^2 > 0$	$time^2 < 0$
U(2,2)	**U(2,2)**
particle no. > 0	particle no. < 0
$time^2 < 0$	$time^2 > 0$

Particles and antiparticles (see the white boxes), hence, will populate the same spacetime area – although the event horizon is between them. A corresponding statement will hold true for the 2 bluish areas against each other.

Let us symbolically sketch the same situation somewhat differently by applying a system of coordinates representing squared CMS-time q = mx (upwards) versus squared heavy mass m (to the right). (In this sketch, the black hole comes to lie at the left-hand side of the vertical event horizon.) The arrows indicate the arrows of ordinary time t (= 0-component of the 4-vector x), which in all 4 quadrants point towards increasing |t|, i.e., towards positive t square in the upper 2 boxes, and towards negative t square in the lower 2 boxes.

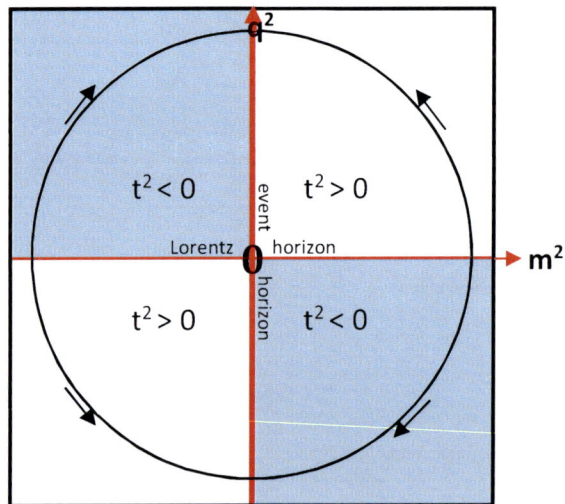

The matter getting lost over the event horizon in our part of the universe will reappear beyond it (inside the black hole region) in terms of an increase of matter there. Due to the reversal of ordinary time, however, this *increase* of matter there (by our view at our side of the event horizon) will be interpreted (by the view of somebody sitting beyond the event horizon) as a *decrease* of antimatter, there.

By these 2 different views, either side will claim its own version of matter or antimatter, respectively, to decrease with increasing time when measured in its own system. In accordance with our observation in the beginning, hence, both sides of the event horizon are absolutely equivalent to each other, indeed.

20. Life in a Black Hole

The part behind an event horizon is called a black hole. Schwarz-schild predicted its existence in 1916 by following Einstein's General Relativity. The application area of this theory, however, ends at the event horizon. His extrapolation beyond it, therefore, was pure phantasy, which runs into an unphysical singularity, indeed.

On the other hand, the presence of corresponding strong gravitational fields, as predicted in front of such an event horizon, has been verified by astronomers. Even the disappearance of matter behind such a limiting horizon has been observed. But Einstein's theory is based on a macroscopic description by differential geometry, which is continuous. Its group-theoretical aspect has been left aside, however.

As demonstrated on preceding pages, group theory – contrary to differential geometry – does allow for a *consistent* extrapolation. The preceding chapter illustrates its logic by following the parity behaviour. Our passage over the event horizon, there, means a rotation by the generator of (the imaginary, reaction-channel variant of) heavy mass within the (4,6)-plane of the conformal group SO(2,4).

Now, Special Relativity is a matter of the dimensions 5, 1, 2, and 3 only. Hence, that (4,6)-transformation will leave **Special Relativity untouched!** However, it will exchange CMS-spacetime and energy-momentum against each other, and, equally, their non-linear variants:

$$\mathbf{Q}_\mu \leftrightarrow \mathbf{P}_\mu$$
$$\mathbf{X}_\mu \leftrightarrow \mathbf{V}_\mu$$

This still might sound unspectacular. But, as we have seen, already,

$$\mathbf{P}_\mu = \mathbf{M}_0 \cdot \mathbf{V}_\mu$$
$$\mathbf{Q}_\mu = \mathbf{M}_0 \cdot \mathbf{X}_\mu$$

Einstein's non-linear, macroscopic spacetime X follows from the linear, microscopic CMS-spacetime Q by constructing the quotient Q/M – and, analogously, the non-linear velocity V from the linear, microscopic energy-momentum P by P/M. Such a ("ray"-) representation, however, will *collect* all (Q,M)-pairs giving the same value of X, and similarly for (P,M) giving V.

As a consequence, the above (Q,P)-exchange will disintegrate Einstein's X-landscape by reordering the former *local* spectrum of physical objects according to their former *velocity* spectrum, and v.v. For astronomers, our old picture of a multitude of disconnected black holes scattered about our continuous sky, after jumping across any of their event horizons, will look like one continuous "**black ocean**" with a multitude of disconnected islands scattered on it, which represent our old world reorganized according to its old velocity spectrum.

Both **partial worlds** – our own world in front of an event horizon and that "black" one behind it – hence, principally look alike; just a couple of parameters are redefined and the course of time is reversed, there. The separation of both partial worlds from each other, though, will have led to an **independent development of history**, here and there. And that independence, at least, will include the creation of our universe (and others), too.

That time reversal at the event horizon and at the Lorentz horizon, both of them present only in the secondary dynamic channel but not in the primary reaction channel, will provide the impression that time development inside all 4 sections of a universe will always proceed away from the big bang, and that matter (like antimatter), in the eyes of *both* sides, (formally) will always fall <u>into</u> an event horizon and will <u>never</u> come <u>out</u> of it. This also agrees with the actual experimental observations. *(Hawking still claimed the opposite. But he could neither prove it substantially, nor did he know QG.)*

On the other hand, this behaviour formally will initialize something similar to a circulation of quanta, which, in the course of time leaves one side of the event horizon in order to enter its opposite side. There, however, matter entering at an early time is reinterpreted as antimatter leaving it at a late time, and v.v.

Now, the event horizon is characterised by its (time-like) energy-momentum becoming equal to a (space-like) spacetime. Squared energy-momentum and squared spacetime, hence, must both vanish there. A glance at our cosmic hyperboloid reveals, however, that its U(2,2)-surface does not satisfy this condition at any (finite) place – as long as we adhere to Einstein's equivalence principle.

In QG, however, this principle is subordinate: inertial and heavy masses vary independently of each other; there are "virtual" masses! The equivalence principle simply fixes its globally most probable value on the statistical average. A transformation with heavy mass will change its inertial mass.

Microscopically, by the dark-energy effect, the event horizon will thus be repulsive (asymptotic approximation only). *Macroscopically*, however, the opposite, gravitational attraction of layered structures will become effective (cf. the next chapter). This will still be enhanced by the overlay of linear CMS-spacetimes Q and heavy masses M provided their quotients Q/M, representing their conventional, non-linear spacetimes, happen to coincide. Separated black holes, thus, will become irresistibly attractive.

In group theory, a spectrum will underlie **selection rules**. In QG, hence, the number of states – i.e., the number of "points" – is drastically diminished with decreasing (absolute) time towards zero; cf. my sketch of "cosmic inflation". This is also ensured by the minimal availability of such Q-values able to contribute to the ray representation of classical spacetime X, there. A rough inspection, hence, will demonstrate some thinning-out effect of the point density existing not only for asymptotically great values of time in our universe but also for distances close to its origin.

On the other hand, a dynamic model like Einstein's GR assumes that our world is the result of a causal development that started out of some "grain of seed" which, in some unknown way, had been present already at the outset of time, i.e., at a "big bang" nobody can explain. By those models, all information should already have been accumulated in that grain and the number of states per time slice should have varied only by group-theoretical reduction processes, since.

A glance at cosmic inflation reveals that the point density in GR with its pointed, local big-bang scenario, then, should be much higher than in our QG reflecting Bell's decentralised, "multi-local" superdeterminism by adding more and more points from Q_9- to Q_9-slice. (Remember that the dynamic channel does not conserve probability!)

The dynamic generators G are defined in a Hermitian way. Their exponential summation exp[iaG], according to Fourier, will give rise to full transformations. In this summation, however, it is multiplied by an additional imaginary factor i. For (the space-like) CMS-location generators, hence, there will be additional imaginary contributions, as well, which are absent for the (time-like) CMS-time generator. Close to the origin, however, those r-number contributions left will be spread rather sparsely; only with some distance, i.e., outside the wasp waist of the cosmic hyperboloid, will they increase again. In both cases, therefore, we will observe a **depletion** of contributions towards the origin.

Only by leaving aside these facts, will the summation of those individual CMS-contributions to give rise to the ray representation of classical spacetime provide the misjudgement of an apparent concentration of matter close to the "big bang" familiar to us by tradition. In contradiction to Einstein's GR with its dynamical, extremely compact big-bang scenario, hence, we rather should assume QG to be depleted of points there. This effective gap between positive and negative times ensures the *macroscopic* commensurability of the event horizon with the Lorentz horizon.

Remark: The mutual exchange of spacetime against 4-momentum and v.v. at the event horizon, when combined with the Lorentz behaviour of space and time, will already be felt far outside the event horizon (i.e., before its "spaghettisation" as it is called in literature) and, last but not least, contribute to an instability of larger matter concentrations leading towards an effective **limitation of size of cosmic objects**.

The classical argument to limit the size of a black hole itself by its light-pressure ("Eddington limit"), due to time reversal at the event horizon, on the other hand, is irrelevant in QG.

As the crucial property of an event horizon, we observe the formal transition to **superluminosity interpreted as spacetime behaviour**! As a result, spacetime and energy-momentum are just 2 sides of the same coin; together, they are components of the same 8-vector.

21. The Causal Gap

The equations of General Relativity <u>can</u> pass the event horizon. This demonstrates that **GR is** a **macroscopic** model indirectly harbouring superpositions of microscopic states among which statistic interpolations are at work which are even (inconsistently) overlapping the event horizon. Microscopically, however, this transition is a privilege either of the reaction channel or, in its **8**-dimensional version, of Quantum Gravity.

For QG, the approach to an event horizon already means a creeping rotation off the time-like energy-momentum towards the space-like CMS-spacetime (and v.v.). This, however, also means a change in the value of its inertial mass: Einstein's equivalence principle is overridden – particle physicists talk of "**virtual**" mass values and states – a strange world to Einstein. The transition itself, then, will be executed at the event horizon.

Anyway: GR, here, is entering a territory forbidden for it. It desperately tries to keep the equivalence principle upright – but falls into the singularity trap, instead. In reality, however, the 8-dimensionality of QG is taking effect. The 3 parities, C, T, and P, are their door openers in the sense of that 3-fold nesting of U(1,1)-spinors, which also allows for being expressed by 3 labels running from 1 to 2, each:

$$\left(\begin{pmatrix}\begin{pmatrix}\blacksquare\\\color{red}\blacksquare\end{pmatrix}\\\begin{pmatrix}\blacksquare\\\color{red}\blacksquare\end{pmatrix}\\\begin{pmatrix}\blacksquare\\\color{red}\blacksquare\end{pmatrix}\end{pmatrix}\right) = (a_{mnk}), \quad m,n,k \in \{1,2\}.$$

Now, at the event horizon, black and red boxes and nesting brackets will be mutually exchanged with each other – by k, hence, *Dirac's spinor* against his antispinor. Related to the 8 dimensions of our *uni-*

verse (cf. below), its analogue would be their split into its 2x4 domains in front of and behind the event horizon, respectively.

Equally, we could apply m or n replacing k for a pair exchange of two spinors – or horizons. Altogether, we would thus arrive at the 8 components of QG, represented by some pair of 4-dimensional spinors or by the corresponding domains on the 8 respective horizon parts in a universe.

We have already discussed the event horizon. The Lorentz-horizon derives from it by a simple mutual exchange of its dimensions 5 and 6. This is mathematics, however. Its physical interpretation is much more sophisticated and unfamiliar: Heavy mass and CMS-time will be exchanged, and the Lorentz booster will do so with momentum. In our 1-shelled cosmic hyperboloid, this will slightly change the content of its Q_9-parameter, and its time-axis will be substituted.

For the 3rd parity P, again, let us start with an *imaginary* rotation, this time within the energy-plane (5,6) still left. This means considering the 2-shelled cosmic hyperboloid we obtain from its 1-shelled variant by the transition to imaginary Q_9:

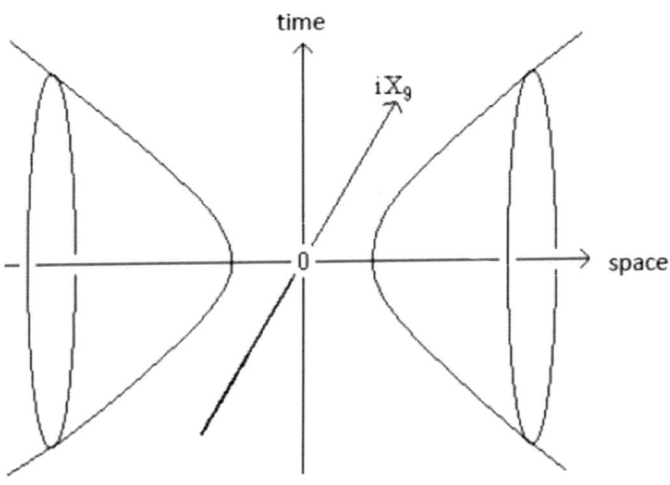

Here, positive and negative space sections are properly separated from each other. A glance at the drawing of our 1-shelled cosmic hyperboloid, however, is less helpful. Thus, in the world formula, that rupture by the event horizon only will be the result from the transition of CMS-spacetime to energy-momentum – and v.v.

The rupture of the Lorentz horizon, then, will result analogously by exchanging the conformal dimensions # 5 and # 6 against each other. That gap by spatial parity P, on the other hand, is obvious from the above 2-shelled variant of our cosmic hyperboloid. Here, the apparent problem, when considering a rotation with an r-number rotation angle within the 1-shelled hyperboloid instead, essentially, is the absence of a corresponding rupture, together with the summation of *microscopic* CMS-spacetime giving rise to Einstein's *classical* spacetime – and all that by applying different criteria to both parts of the event horizon, in addition. In the next chapter, we shall avoid that "mess" by applying the above labels m,n,k, which clearly separate the domains.

As we observed already, forces enter physics by ripping, stretching, and squeezing the previously even distribution of points on the surface of a sphere representing the reaction channel into the distorted distribution of its dynamic channel. An ("entropic") **force**, then, is the (negative) gradient of that new distribution. This effect is especially obvious with dark energy, which, in the global scale of our universe, accelerates matter (and antimatter) towards its outside.

Now, a competitive effect is gravity. It is predominantly an effect that acts locally, on local mass aggregations. A particle running in parallel to a layered arrangement will be deflected from its straight propagation towards the denser layer because it will meet more resistance there and will therefore cover less distance per time. Effectively gravity and dark energy are thus acting into opposite directions.

Let us, therefore, keep this in mind: **Gravity is a deflection** from its tangential course towards a higher density, and **dark energy is an acceleration** in the radial direction towards lower densities. The asymptotic radius of a universe will be roughly destined by the balance of both forces. "Internal" forces will provide additional contributions; however, their ranges are much shorter (but stronger). A particle radius, thus, will be destined by a *corresponding* interplay.

22. The Mater-Mundi Principle

The **matryoshka** principle is still some vague suggestion that hierarchies of various differing orders of magnitude could well be nesting into each other in nature. Now, the mater-mundi principle quite precisely presents an explicit example of how, on a cosmic scale, our world could be incorporated as some "**super-quant**" into a "**super-world**" of equal structure, indeed, i.e., into a "**mater mundi**" (Latin for "mother of the world").

As demonstrated in the preceding three chapters, the 3 parities, C, T, and P, on a macroscopic level, globally separate our world by its event horizon, its Lorentz horizon, and its causal gap into $2**3 = 8$ sections, altogether. As a "super-quant", our world, thus, will give rise to 8 components. A multiverse consisting of some multitude of worlds, then, will represent a collection of some multitude of super-quants each of which is composed of 8 components.

On the microscopic level, however, these three parities are not commensurable with each other; depending on the channel, they are generating an SU(2) or an SU(1,1) configuration, respectively. Provided we again denote their SO(2,1)-dimensions by 6,5,4, then the remaining SO(2,4)-dimensions k=3,2,1 will stay undisturbed. But a simple Lorentz booster (5,k) will already blur the boundaries of the blocks because, by its mixing of 5 with k, it will indirectly introduce that 5 by means of the k into linear momentum (6,k) and CMS-location (4,k) as well.

Last but not least, this will mix all those separate 3 parity ranges with each other again: In other words: Those $2**3 = 8$ components are not really independent of each other, in fact; i.e., those 8 components represent an "**irreducible**" supervector in 8 dimensions! Particle physicists like to call a particle whose extension is too small to be measured a "point particle". It accumulates all its properties to just 1 single (gross) value per super-component.

From some "higher-level" perspective, our "supervector" would again degenerate into some quite ordinary vector. A single vector of this kind could be rotated so that it points in just one of the 8 directions. Depending on that specific direction, we could distinguish 8 types of those "super-quants" (with respect to the coordinate system given).

This individual rotation, however, will not "diagonalise" all super-quants simultaneously: Other super-quants will point into different directions; they will need their own, individual rotations. Quantum models here introduce the concept of "**non-distinguishability**" meaning that the *components* of all super-quants belonging to the *same* global direction are treated equally (up to individual normalisation factors).

This non-distinguishability postulate, however, is a **philosophical problem**. It means that all components of the <u>same global class</u> (= type) of the super-quants (up to normalisation factors) are treated in their **symmetrised** forms only.

Mathematically, this means that all "equal super-quants", separately <u>within each of the 8 classes</u>, are interpreted to have been subject to a **selection process** where they were all lined up in a sequence irrespective of their order within that sequence. ("Take 2 yellow, 9 blue, 5 red, and 3 green marbles out of a bag". Only the order <u>of colours</u> is considered.)

Young-Tableaux treat these problems explicitly in their extended spin-addition theorems, but fans of classical functional analysis often like to shirk these group-theoretical problems. Usually, they accept only totally symmetric "boson" representations (**Bose-Einstein statistics**) and totally antisymmetric "fermion" representations (**Fermi-Dirac statistics**); mixed-symmetric structures are a red rag for them. For particle physics, however, this spin-statistics theorem is irrelevant (cf. our Chapter 38).

By its invention of a "2nd quantisation", the "Standard" Model of particles took over Fermi-Dirac statistics for fermions to particle physics as well, although Gell-Mann's baryons satisfy mixed-symmetric "internal" statistics. Hence, in order to "correct nature", functional analysts invented a quantum number "colour", in addition. Artificially enforcing the spin-statistics theorem by that method to domains not suited for it, however, they made Dirac's model mathematically inconsistent by equipping it with superfluous singularities. QG strictly avoids those inadequate symmetry patterns. (In QG, fermions are organised according to the "shell model".)

Now, those super-quants, in principle, will all result in differing sizes. Long-term collisions will largely have levelled those varying sizes statistically. The above symmetrisations of "equal" super-quants, then, will have mediated the rest of "equality" to them. "Identical" super-quanta will thus have become effectively indistinguishable, indeed.

(In order to prevent confusion: All those statistical compensation processes do not take place within a temporal relation needing respective reaction times, but they do so timelessly, i.e., in terms of effects conserving consistency according to Bell's superdeterminism!)

The same effect will be expected one level below, as well: As "super-quants" of a different, next lower level our experimentalists actually have no idea of, our original, simple quanta will have adapted to each other according to a similar method. As just mentioned, this levelling process will not be a temporal process, though – time only will be *generated* by these quanta! – but it will be some more abstract process generating consistency according to Bell's superdeterminism.

Now, these 3 parity doublings can hardly be separated from each other: Provided we ignore the domain behind the event horizon, e.g., then the gravitational effect of the black holes will be missing in our part of the universe, as well!

23. Quark Confinement

All **3 parity doublings** will thus have to remain present for <u>every</u> one of the 8 super-quants. When transferred from a level below our own quanta to our quanta, this is that ill-reputed "**quark confinement**" of *our* world: an implicit irreducibility condition requiring quanta (of equal k) to show up only in multiples of 3.

That quark confinement is an immediate consequence of the 3 nesting levels of dynamic U(1,1)-spinors giving those 2**3 = 8 dimensions of our world. These 3 (inseparable) parities only complete Einstein's 4-dimensional world towards the world we are living in, in fact. It is ironic that these parities, as shown, are transferred to us from the matryoshka level below our own level. Thus, they represent a surprising witness of another world, indeed.

At our level, then, we identify them in terms of additional, "**internal**" parameters l,r,t – in addition to those m,n,k of our own spinors (cf. chapter "The Causal Gap"):

$$a_{mnk} \quad \rightarrow \quad a_{mnk;lrt} \; .$$

Each of these parameters m to t has 2 values: "up" and "down". For ordinary spin, m, this is familiar to us. n doubles it to Dirac's spinor, and the 2 k-values, then, doube it another time to give QG. We identify that additional "l" as an "**isospin**", e.g. This doubling of the number 3 of labels will give rise to a configuration of dimension 8x8 = 64. In the dynamic channel, this is a U(32,32). Our world, obviously, represents an "internal" singlet component.

Depending on which one of these time- or space-like dimensions we collect to give a 2-dimensional sub-configuration, we obtain a U(2) or a U(1,1) for each of these labels. But we do not know that a priori. Hence, we have to rely on some ansatz, comparing it with the experimental situation we are meeting.

However, from our own QG, we know quite well that for a meson like the graviton (or the photon, or the pion, …), particle number – represented by the label k, there – should vanish. Because in QG every quant will result in (plus or minus) 1 unit, those "internal" parameters should all assemble together to form some "internal" singlet for the graviton.

Considered from the point of view of the order of their labels within a quant, this triplet of "internal" parameters is some set in 3 dimensions allowing for being organised in terms of an SU(3). Now, mathematics will become sophisticated; the untrained layman should probably skip this passage. The expert will find details at the end of Chapter 30:

According to group theory, the above SU(3)-singlet will be represented by a totally antisymmetric pattern which, as an S-group, is mathematically equivalent to a so-called "trace singlet". The older people among us will well remember it from the early days of Gell-Mann's quark model. At that time, just 3 types of quarks were known. Now, a ("customary") meson is assumed to be the product of one quark and one antiquark.

In Gell-Mann's old SU(3)-model, this gives 3x3 = 9 mesons: an octet plus just that "trace singlet". These 8 octet mesons arise from the original ninefold product by subtracting 1/3 of the unit matrix. Now, it is exactly that factor 1/3 which, last but not least, will give rise to the "internal" quantum numbers to be a multiple of 1/3 as we observe it in case of the particle number N of a quant.

Those 8 diagonal "internal" quantum numbers are usually collected to pairs of opposite values. By subtracting this trace singlet from the pair (+1,−1) we obtain (+2/3,−4/3), which by the factor 1/2 will change to (+1/3,−2/3) – the well-known charge values (up to signs and the order) of the electromagnetic interaction in the "standard" model of elementary particles.

So much for justifying the *need* for the **quark confinement**, which, hence, proves to be an additional **consistency condition for** a representation to be **irreducible**. (Its duty is, to prevent the artificial separation of black holes from our own partial world.)

For its technical enforcement, cf. Chapter 25. Due to its group-theoretical double structure – 8 components for QG, but just 3 for the number of its labels, however – it is not at all trivial even to justify its mere existence by theory. Thus, it is not surprising why, in the official literature trimmed for economic efficiency, the quark confinement has remained an unsolved puzzle until nowadays, whose proper decoding had been reserved to QG.

24. Unified Field Theories

We just observed ("quark confinement") that the description of our quanta still ignores the **"internal" octet** of the 3 parity doublings: Every quant of QG should occur in 8 "internal" variants, each. As mentioned already, the total number of dimensions will then increase from 8 in QG to 8x8 = 64 in **"New Physics"**, and the total number of its generators from 8x8 = 64 to 64x64 = 4096. Let me indicate them by some square array:

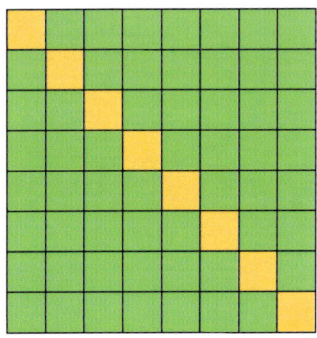

The diagonal elements (in yellow) are indicating the 8 "internal" Quantum Gravities thus generated; they are independent of each other:

$$U(8)_1 \oplus U(8)_2 \oplus U(8)_3 \oplus \dots \oplus U(8)_8 \subset U(64).$$

The total number of their generators, is **8x**(8x8) = 512. The 4096–512 = 3584 (green) generators left, then, relate those 8 "internal" Quantum Gravities with each other; they *transfer* them into each other. Altogether, these 4096 (green + yellow) generators represent the **"Grand Unified Theory"** **GUT** of all "internal" forces of nature.

As mentioned already, that additional configuration pattern ensures the common presence of all 3 parity doublings by certain quantum numbers to be multiples of 1/3 – more precisely: some pairs (+1/2,–1/2) will transform to **(+2/3,–1/3)**. This is the form the "quark confinement" once became known by.

On the other hand, this division into thirds still splits off an additional, 9th QG as an "internal" singlet from our GUT-octet. In literature, a combination of the "internal" forces (i.e., of our octet) with gravity (i.e., with this "internal" singlet) somewhat pompously is called a "**Theory of Everything**" (**ToE**).

But literature is dominated by *functional analysts*, as stated already, and Einstein's *differential geometry* is just is a part of it. *Infinities* are their daily bread. Configurations there are usually confounded with "*symmetries*". According to that artificial agreement, the GUT is considered there as some *asymptotic* property to be approximated only by high energies. Thus, people have been able to correlate the electrodynamic force to the weak force, and they hope that experiments soon will be adding the strong force, in addition. However, *there* is no hope to include gravity, as well.

Contrary to this, *our* above GUT gets along without asymptotics; those various forces are converted into each other by simple rotations in a U(64) or U(32,32) system, respectively – gravity included. The rest, then, "just" will be a matter of normalisations. –

Let me add a hint to the expert: The parities of QG allow for an analogous transfer to the "internal" octet. In order to distinguish those new T and C from the old ones, let us denote them by T' and C', respectively. According to Pauli's matrices 1 and 2, particle physics separates 2 types of products. They are called

Hermitian conjugation: $\quad T \otimes T', \quad C \otimes C'.$

In QG, T and C relate the 2 sections on both sides of the event horizon and of the Lorentz horizon, respectively. In particle physics, C also represents Dirac's gamma-matrix # 0 in the scalar product of the vector calculus. T' and C' are doing so one level deeper, below our "quanta".

25. Range Horizons

A density is some number of elements per space available (in a linear context: 1/r law). In New Physics, these "elements" are simply quanta (of the type considered). This is its **microscopic** aspect. According to that, a force is defined by its negative gradient (definition of a **repulsive**, **entropic force**). Dark energy is an example.

Macroscopically, these quanta are combined as elementary particles. By the generator (3,4), such a compound is "extended". If you tear at one of its edges, you will draw the entire compound behind you. Provided this compound is spread over zones of varying densities, the majority of these quanta, usually, will find themselves in zones different from those that single quant picked out will have its origin in. Macroscopically, some density distribution will be present.

Layered zones will *rotate* that compound in such a way that it will change its course from zones of lower densities towards zones of higher densities. This related *peripheral*, apparent force opposite to the *radial*ly repulsive force generated by entropy will then be that force we are **macroscopic**ally interpreting as being **attractive**. As examples, let me mention gravity or the cohesive effect that keeps a particle together.

Those so-called "internal" forces of nature that give rise to electromagnetism or to the nuclear forces, i.e., to our octet forces, belong to the latter type of forces. Microscopically, they are directed towards their outsides; in their compound forms, they are commuted to macroscopic forces which are effectively directed towards their insides.

Their outer limit is the gravitational range of gravity, i.e., the size of our universe. The density of quanta contributing to an "internal" force, then, is their (effective) number divided by that size of our universe. On the other hand, that "number" is a measure for the range of that force. As a result, there will be different **range horizons** for the individual forces.

The effective radius of a particle will therefore depend on the type of force considered. For gravity, i.e., for our "internal" singlet, all quanta contribute (with the same sign). The 8 "internal" octet forces, on the other hand, result from a 3-fold horizon nesting (2**3 = 8). Provided all quanta would be diagonalised with respect to all of their 8 charge types, then we would observe great densities (horizon ranges) for the "internal" quantum numbers Q (electric charge) and T ("triality" = "strong" nuclear charge), e.g., but small ones for Λ or E (which, both, still will have to be defined).

Observe for the range that a force field multiplies 2 factors. From gravity or from the electric Coulomb force we know their dependence on the inverse squared distance deriving from its potential (= density) 1/r. There, however, (from solving the "Klein-Gordon equation") an exponential factor still adds, which originates from the mass of the respective exchange particle (graviton, photon, pion, etc.):

$$\text{Yukawa force:} \quad \mathbf{F} \propto \pm \frac{1}{r^2} \cdot \mathbf{e^{-m \cdot r}} \quad \text{(with c=1=\hbar).}$$

The respective Yukawa force is an approximation to these orders of magnitude. For massive exchange particles, this Yukawa width defines the force range; for massless particles like the photon, it is the (unlimited) Coulomb width. The transition probability, however, is a mere "Clebsch-Gordon coefficient". Contrary to the situation with the massless photon, the tiny gravitational constant will give rise to the existence of some tiny **little graviton mass**.

The strength of a force depends on its density gradient, in the Yukawa case, hence, on its peak width. Within its range horizon, thus, it will be stronger for the less common types of quanta and weaker for the more current types. (Here, I briefly have to anticipate the next chapter, according to which the octet ranges are still drastically shortened again.) As that "internal" singlet is touching all quanta, **gravity**, in accordance to experiment, thus, will be the by far **weakest** of all **forces**.

The graviton, which is still waiting for its experimental discovery *as a particle*, by definition (!) does not contribute to the octet forces. Here, we observe the typical chicken-and-egg situation: Do the forces define the particle spectrum, or does the particle spectrum define the types of forces? This problem still is unsolved. Actually, I personally tend to believe the following concept:

By its ToE version, the GUT defines how to nest 9 = 8+1 variants of QG (commuting with each other) which, each by itself and independently of each other, by its linear Casimir operator carries one specific, "internal" quantum number, each. For the (trace-)singlet, this number is called "**particle number**", for the remaining 8 octets "**charge**". Sum and difference of any two of those nonets represent a chiral pair, as we are familiar with from the **minimal coupling** of electrodynamics to ordinary dynamics.

Together with the dynamical singlets, this pair altogether will consist of **9 chiral components** *(cf. Chapter 30, especially its matrix U converting the 8 octet representations into their chiral representations – pulling the singlet along like a trailer. [8], then, relates them to the combinations observed by experiment, as laid down in our Chapter 30).*

According to the previous chapter, each of the 4 (C,T)-quadrants are again quadrupling. For each of these now 16 (CxC',TxT')-quadrants of our chiral U(32,32), hence, there will result one chiral QG of type U(4x8,4x8) whose particle content will have to satisfy Bells superdeterminism consistently. In this sense, those 8 to 9 types of forces would primarily fix the secondary particle spectrum, and it would be the task of theoreticians consistently to supplement the constraints still open in accordance with experiment.

This way, it could well turn out that the graviton of spin 2 the theoreticians actually expect to exist is not there at all and that its properties are merely some collective effect resulting from quite different properties of QG. Analogously, the photon might be at disposal in its position as "the" mediator of electrodynamics. Under general-relativistic conditions, New Physics could grossly give rise to an entire spectrum of states reproducing the properties of electrodynamics – in addition to the photon!

The world formula of QG still adds a non-locality in terms of a linear **oscillator potential** to those Yukawa potentials. In its force centre it will vanish; with distance it will accelerate the particle towards the speed of light. In the case of rejection, it will tear the particle to pieces beyond its effective range. (We are familiar with that effect, already, from passing the event horizon one level higher.)

In order to be able to pass that charge-specific horizon as some self-contained particle, all charges of the respective charge type will have to add up to zero. By doing so, for this special force type, its point of attack will disappear. For a baryon consisting of 3 quarks carrying the "strong" charges $T = +2/3$, $-1/3$, and another $-1/3$ (compare Chapter 30) this is just satisfied. Historically, this was the source of postulating the existence of something like a quark confinement, which QG, then (see above), identified as an irreducibility condition. – Another line of argumentation in favour was that the electric charge Q of a particle always proved to be an integer value. Without that quark confinement with respect to T, odd multiples of 1/3 would present themselves for Q, as well.

The "standard" model of elementary particles, finally, defined a particle to be a **hadron** provided it could be interpreted as composed purely of quarks defined by those 3 values of N (= particle number), T, and Q (beside isospin and "flavours").

Leptons, the photon, the graviton, the W-mesons, and plenty of more particles still need additional charge types; the "standard" model, hence, separates them by the argument that "they are not composed of quarks". Well, QG is proving the opposite: all matter, if "dark" or "light", is composed purely of our quanta and of nothing else.

26. How Particles Condense Out of Dark Matter

However our universe might have arisen from the billiards of quanta and universes – in the ideal case, microscopically, it should be a component of an irreducible representation of quanta. Such a component will be the result of so and so many quanta of some particular type, each. Depending on the direction of diagonalisation, it could take the form of an irreducible superposition of such components belonging to the *same* irreducible gross representation, as well.

With 8x8 = 64 types of quanta only, inevitably the majority of their unimaginably large number will locally gather to singlets, as well. As the number of dimensions of our universe is a multiple of 2, it will allow for knitting such a singlet out of single *pairs of quanta*. The 64 (linear) quantum numbers of those partners, then, will be equal but will carry opposite signs *(technical realisation: in QG by connecting them by charge conjugation C, in the Dirac formalism by the matrix gamma-zero)*. Mathematically, we will then get the singlet by summing all those 64 pair types.

Provided we are summing only those 8 "internal" variables but not their Dirac content, then, last but not least, we are left with just those $(2+2) \times (2+2) = 16$ combinations of Dirac's a- and b-spins (summed over the 8 "internal" variants):

$$a^+_{i'} b^+_{i''} , a^+_{i'} a^-_{i''} , b^-_{i'} b^+_{i''} , b^-_{i'} a^-_{i''} .$$

But what are these 4 pair types telling us physically? Formally, they look like particles; however, they have no non-valence parts (cf. below). In that sense, they *are* **not particles**. Just remember: In QG, spacetime and momentum are quantities defined in the macrocosm; only by statistical superpositions (i.e., by applying the law of great numbers) will they become measurable at all.

Now, by experiment, the quantum numbers of QG are of a rather different "**rigidity**": Some of them allow for a quite simple variation – their 3 components of space or momentum, e.g. – others, however, like lepton number, e.g., are effectively not variable at all. The two spin components admit a relatively easy switch into each other. When extending the above 4 pair types by their spin dependence, in addition, their number will be multiplied by 2x2 = 4 giving 4x4 = 16.

The characteristic feature of these 16 entities is:

- They are **gravitationally active**: Half of them carry (plus or minus 2 units of) **energy**.
- They are **polarisable**: They represent 4 **spin** singlets plus 4 spin triplets.
- Similarly, they carry 4 variants of <u>CMS</u>-space; but Einstein's conventional space Q/M is not diagonal because the law of great numbers is not applicable to just 2 quanta (in Q or in M, respectively). Hence, those 16 entities are **not localisable**.
- However, **major accumulations** of them are sometimes **approximately localisable**.

These points are just what astronomers define to be the effect of **dark matter**. Those 16 entities, thus, are the *basic* bricks of dark matter *globally* defined by the 3rd- and 4th-order Casimirs of the world formula in Dirac's 4 (dynamical) dimensions. For, by total spin and total booster

$$\vec{\tilde{L}} \equiv \vec{L} + \vec{X} \times \vec{P},$$
$$\vec{\tilde{M}} \equiv \vec{M} + \left(\vec{X}P_0 - X_0\vec{P}\right)$$

the leading terms of the two Casimirs are

$$C_{SU(2,2)}^{(3)} \propto \left(\vec{\tilde{L}} \cdot \vec{\tilde{M}}\right) M_0 \quad + \dots,$$
$$C_{SU(2,2)}^{(4)} \propto \left(\vec{\tilde{M}}^2 - \vec{\tilde{L}}^2\right) M_0^{\,2} + \dots.$$

By decreasing total spin and total booster, hence, heavy mass will increase, and v.v. In practice, these rather abstract changes are reproduced by the above 16 types of pair quanta of dark matter or by the non-valence parts (see below).

The creation of dark matter will stop by itself as soon as the first of the 8 "internal" types of quanta is exhausted, i.e., as soon as additional neutral bricks of the 4x4 types in the above table cannot be constructed anymore. This state will be achieved when all 4 Dirac components of one particular "internal" type of quanta are not available anymore. The world accessible to us outside dark matter then will still dispose on 64–4 = 60 distinguishable quanta only.

Nevertheless, neutral quantum pairs are still allowed to be constructed, only their 8-dimensional summation does not work anymore. When still ignoring them, in addition, we will be left with more sophisticated constructs; these are the **valence parts** of particles. Those "internally" neutral pairs of quanta not absorbed in dark matter will now attach to these valence parts taking them as condensation germs (dipole effect) – like water molecules in the atmosphere of our earth to airborne dust.

They constitute the non-valence structure of elementary particles raining out of dark matter clouds. Like exceptional noble-gas inclusions in crystals, however, a non-valence part sometimes still may include a few dark-matter inclusions.

An elementary particle will thus be some compound uniting a valence with a non-valence part. As far as a particle can be considered as irreducible at all (see Chapter 13), a non-valence and a valence part together are no simple product but an irreducible construct (summing up such products according to certain rules of mathematics, see Chapter 6). The measurability of spacetime, mass, and momentum in Einstein's conventional sense will need a huge number of quantum pairs per particle. In spite of that, the share of "visible matter", by construction ("leftover"), will stay small when compared with that of dark matter.

27. Salty Universes

A particle is an assembly of quanta containing a few valence quanta within a huge number of non-valence quanta. The latter saturate each other in pairs with respect to their "internal" properties. Mathematically, they are organised according to Young tableaux.

Particles represent some intermediate structure between quanta and universes. Their components in terms of tensor labels form "internally" neutral substructures. One level higher, on the level of universes, this corresponds to their saturation with respect to all 3 parities – C, T, and P – in pairs. In addition, those parity-saturated pairs of universes are accumulated to even much more numerous assemblies corresponding to Young tableaux a level lower.

Altogether, provided that physics on that higher level is the same as inside our own world, we arrive at the statement that our universe – black holes and the times before the big bang included – should be part of some narrow multiverse we are embedded in.

In the experiment, this would mean that, on the one hand, dark energy proves the curvature of our own universe; on the other hand, however, that the cosmic background radiation of 3° K we receive from all directions is overlapped by that of all universes surrounding us. As in the interior of a crystal of table salt with its periodically alternating charges, the more remote world around us would give us the impression that it is continuous and flat.

This flatness of space is exactly what astronomers report to us: The measured long-term **flatness of space** combined with the curvature of space of our own universe well documented within its limits **is the experimental evidence of** its embedment into some much larger **multiverse**.

That theoretically asymptotic thinning-out effect of our universe towards its outskirts, when transferred to those surrounding additional universes, in accordance with experiment, will involve the background radiation intruding from outside is largely conserving its frequency spectrum without giving rise to an additional Doppler shift.

The total background radiation we are receiving will hence have to be interpreted as a superposition of some large variety of contributions from universes surrounding us! Compared with the size of our own universe, that tremendously wide environment will appear to us as infinitely large. This will imply that the total structure measured by the background radiation to be effectively flat within the multiverse will appear as a curved partial structure when measured by distances within our own universe.

Cosmologists consider this type of a multiverse structure as an **eternal inflation**. They do not reduce that effect to static Young tableaux. Instead, they attribute it to a dynamically overshooting cosmic inflation accompanied by a continuous creation and split-off of "**bubbles**" to develop themselves to autonomous universes. Thus their model insists on the old big-bang scenario not understood.

This bubble model of eternal inflation lacks our approximately periodic, crystalline structure of individual universes resulting from a Young-type organisation within its multiverse. In analogy with the elementary particles of our own universe and their grouping to macroscopic objects, in an even larger scale, we shall have to understand the distribution of universes to multiverses of some first order (elementary particles) and a distribution of those multiverses of first order to multiverses of some second order (molecules, chemical materials), etc. like sand on a tropical beach: Particles group into atoms, atom group into molecules, molecules into quartz crystals, which then spread amorphously as sand over large regions. But there still will be much more in the world than just this one, desolate, sandy desert!

28. System of Natural Units

Our U(2,2) contains exactly 4 directions commuting with each other, expressed by the O(2,4)-Generators (1,2), (3,4), (5,6) and their linear Casimir. By our human senses, however, evolution did not primarily provide access to the microscopic directions to be used in the reaction channel but rather to the secondary, macroscopic directions (1,2), (3,5), (4,6) together with the linear Casimir to be used in the dynamic channel. Historically, all 4 directions had been normalised independently of each other.

The first two directions, spin$_3$ = (1,2) and the booster$_3$ = (3,5), are the diagonal components of the Lorentz group SO(1,3). They define 2 of the 4 normalisations: **Planck's constant** for spin and the **speed of light** relating the Lorentz booster, (3,5), to spin, (1,2). In fundamental physics, both constants of nature, speed of light and Planck's number, for simplicity reasons, usually are set equal to 1:

$$c = 1 = \hbar.$$

Due to the bilinearity of the generators, the dimensions # 1,2,3,5 normalised according to this way, give rise to entire Special Relativity Theory to become free of further normalisations. However, the dimensions #4 and #6 of QG are still left open. Due to their smallness, however, their *quantised units*, actually, evade being fixed. We could tentatively relate Einstein's conventional spacetime to the waist radius of our cosmic hyperboloid; heavy mass, then, would need an additional parameter. But energy-momentum, as an inverse length, will then be redundant. Hence, the normalisations read:

$$P'_\mu \equiv \frac{1}{\mp} P_\mu$$
$$Q'_\mu \equiv \mp q\, Q_\mu$$
$$D \equiv q\, M_0$$

(The new, normalised units are on the left, the old units normalised to the number of single quanta on the right. D also is known as "dilatation".)

From the postulated smallness of these 3 parameters together with the absence of a blue term in the Klein-Gordon equation (below) we obtain the restrictions

$$|\mathsf{q}| \ll 1/|\mathsf{f}| \ll 1 \ll |\mathsf{f}^2 \mathsf{q}| .$$

Now, the SU(2,2)-Casimir contained in the 2nd-order world formula is the Pythagorean sum of the 15 generators quoted in Chapter 8 (without particle number and with the time-like terms carrying an additional minus factor, cf. Chapter 10):

$$C^{(2)}_{SU(2,2)} \equiv + \left(P_0{}^2 - \vec{P}^2 - M_0{}^2 \right) - \left(Q_0{}^2 - \vec{Q}^2 \right) - \left(\vec{M}^2 - \vec{L}^2 \right).$$

The \$1000 question deferred so far is: Why did nobody write down this simple identity before?

The answer is given by the above dark-blue table: After inserting its 3 orange measuring units, our Casimir above adds 3 terms of totally different orders of magnitude; nobody could imagine that those 3 terms, so different, could have to do anything with each other in order to give rise to a common expression! For Einstein, the equivalence principle (in red) was some feature in addition to but separate from Special Relativity (in pink) — and his non-linear spacetime $X_\mu = Q_\mu/M_0$ even seemed to be something completely different!

Thus, for his General Relativity, Einstein declared the above red term to become the ultimate truth of physics that nobody ever should touch. Nevertheless, he returned to his spacetime concept of Special Relativity trying to boost it towards some more general form. By applying his equivalence principle, however, he found that his spacetime X of Special Relativity could not be kept diagonal any more. He managed that case multiplicatively by introducing some non-constant metric instead of simply adding the blue spacetime terms to his red equivalence terms.

That grand detour enabled him to recognise that the energy-momentum and heavy mass of his equivalence theorem being kept sacrosanct affected his spacetime X of Special Relativity as well (in the well-known differential-geometric way). QG simply is using the direct way by setting the above Casimir equal to constant (world formula).

Einstein applied the multiplicative procedure of a variable metric to find out that the measuring units of the above blue spacetime terms should be extremely small, when compared with those of the red and pink terms. The direct way of understanding it, however, is roughly to acknowledge that the Klein-Gordon equation apparently does not need it; hence, it should be negligibly small. But afterwards, people are usually more experienced, of course.

This Casimir demonstrates in an especially simple way how an increase of heavy mass, e.g., might be compensated in GR by an increase of space – a transformation property not present in Special Relativity. Only, Einstein complicated this simple fact by dispensing it with irreducibility and constructing reducible mixtures of various states showing that this gross compound appeared to satisfy the property desired – a way to create a model introducing the well-known singularities not needed into the interior of a black hole.

As there are additional terms in the above 2nd-order Casimir, Einstein's equivalence principle cannot be true absolutely – as we experienced already. Its definition depends on the relative magnitudes of the 3 measuring units applied to the 3 above terms. Our dark-blue table in the beginning of this chapter quotes them in our human spacetime region.

Further away in our universe (closer to bigger mass assemblies) or closer to the production source of virtual particle states (fluctuating across microscopic event horizons), their definition will provide values that differ from those above because Einstein dogmatically overlooked the independence of heavy mass from inertial mass.

For a stable particle close to the event horizon, the above red and blue contributions to the Casimir vanish. Without the octet forces, thus, the (invariant) quadratic SU(2,2)-Casimir will converge to the pink Lorentz-Casimir, in the spinless case, hence, towards the (negative) squared Lorentz booster.

The compatibility of our 1-shelled cosmic hyperboloid (waist radius positive) with experimental evidence (dark energy repulsive), then, proves that the spin of our universe does not vanish.

29. Coordinate Systems

The formalism of group theory defines a tensor (**Young frame**) composed of components (**Young tableaux**). But a tensor needs some transformation behaviour in order to be defined properly. In the dynamic channel of QG, this means satisfying a U(4,4) – or, in Dirac's truncated version, a U(2,2). Such a transformation allows for introducing some coordinate system. QG fixed it to be a Cartesian system (fitted with some bent metric originating from the world formula). The **diagonalisation** of a quantum, then, means some (pseudo-unitary) "rotation" of that coordinate system that is conserving its metric.

Now, in pseudo-unitary dynamics, time-like <u>and</u> space-like directions coexist side by side, while in the unitary reaction channel only space-like or only time-like directions are present. Provided all measuring units are equal, the reaction channel then describes the surface of a sphere, and we could introduce spherical coordinates based on the trigonometrical functions cos and sin. In the dynamic channel, however, we would need hyperbolic coordinates, instead, which are based on cosh and sinh in order to relate a time-like to a space-like coordinate. These functions are just (half) the sum or difference, respectively, of exponential functions:

$$\textbf{cos, sin :} \quad \propto (e^{+ix} \pm e^{-ix}) \quad ,$$
$$\textbf{cosh, sinh:} \quad \propto (e^{+x} \pm e^{-x}) = T \pm 1/T.$$

Observe that – contrary to the upper spherical case with its imaginary exponents – in the lower, hyperbolic case, the exponents are r-numbers, whose absolute values, T and 1/T, are inverse to each other. By applying an **exponential measuring scale** – cosh and sinh – to replace the linear measuring scale of the generators we obtain some coordinate system that is more adapted to handling the opposing time-like coordinate vs. its space-like counterpart, while a related space-like pair or a related time-like pair could maintain its relative trigonometric coordinates transforming cos vs. sin.

The cosmic hyperboloid might serve as an example. Its hyperbolic outward distortion will show itself in terms of an asymptotic decrease of the **quantum density** when we approach the outskirts of our universe. The discrete structure of its quanta allows us to cut off its size after having passed its last quantum. A totally analogous line of argumentation will hold when we are going to determine the **radius of an elementary particle** with respect to a certain type of its interactions.

This exponential **thinning-out effect**, however, also will happen asymptotically for extremely short distances. In this case, it is the trigonometric radius which, by a limited number of quanta, will converge towards a minimal value of quantum density when it is reduced in size. (Compare it with what I mentioned with respect to the macroscopic commutativity at about the event and Lorentz horizons close to the origin of our universe).

As a final result, we should keep in mind that a measurement ranging far enough outside from our human existence on earth, without us being conscious of it, might yield essentially different scaling properties, that is to say an exponential measuring system that we are not aware of applying. And this thinning-out effect might occur at extremely great or extremely small distances, as well (asymptotically pushing back (x to exp[x]) the outside limits of our universe (maximum = exp[+x]) towards plus infinity, and its microscopic sensitivity, i.e., its inside limits (minimum = exp[−x]) towards a distance of zero corresponding to x = minus infinity).

Thus, we observe that the continuous infinitesimal calculus, first of all, will basically start from an equal distribution of its points x on its axis in order to vary a position x on it by an amount of dx, while its discrete variant of group theory will first of all have to bother about the definition of distances (distortion) between two neighbouring points.

These two different points of view might rapidly end up in an incompatible discrepancy in the measuring systems applied (in the above thinning-out example: logarithmic vs. linear)! Thus, a singular Yukawa or Coulomb potential of a continuous model, due to its metric, might easily convert to a non-singular form in a discrete model by combining the thinning-out effect with the cut-off effect of its quanta.

The combination of differently scaled coordinates to 2-dimensional shells ("planes") will be subject to additional (elliptic) distortions giving rise to additional, lateral shear forces. These are those shear forces which, asymptotically towards the event horizon, give rise to **admixtures of heavy mass to CMS-time**, until, finally, heavy mass totally takes over the helm (sin =1). In the end, however, the combined norm of heavy mass and CMS-time will vanish completely at the event horizon.

30. Charges

Let us denote the 8 diagonal parameters (cf. table, upper line) of the "internal" structures according to their powers of 2 (8 = 2**3) by means of 3 labels (1 = up, 2 = down; i = ordinary spin component). These diagonal parameters are the "**charges**":

	N	Q	T	L	Λ	E	A	M
a^+_{i211}	+⅓	+⅔	−⅓	0	0	0	0	0
a^+_{i111}	+⅓	−⅓	−⅓	0	0	0	0	0
a^+_{i222}	+⅓	+⅔	+⅔	0	0	0	+½	+½
a^+_{i122}	+⅓	−⅓	+⅔	0	0	0	+½	−½
a^+_{i212}	+⅓	+⅔	−⅓	−½	−½	0	0	0
a^+_{i112}	+⅓	−⅓	−⅓	−½	+½	0	0	0
a^+_{i221}	+⅓	+⅔	+⅔	+½	0	+½	−½	0
a^+_{i121}	+⅓	−⅓	+⅔	+½	0	−½	−½	0

The corresponding 3 labels I,j,k of dynamics, somewhat chaotically, were written by Dirac as i = 1,2 in terms of lower labels, j = a,b in terms of labelled entities, and k=+,− in terms of upper labels (cf. table, left-hand column for (jk) = (a⁺). Those 8x8 = 64 entries are not a result of theory but of a pragmatic interpretation of the experimental data (respecting the orthogonality of the related states, see below). For (jk) = (b⁺), all charges will change their signs. For the moment this should be a sufficient description of the technical details.

Physical literature only knows 3 types of "internal" forces besides gravity: The "strong" nuclear force (corresponding to the above quantum number T), the electromagnetic force (Q), and the "weak" nuclear force. The latter might be *symbolised* by L, above. From QG, however, we find that the **"weak" force** is not reproduced by some monopole but by some **dipole force** – hence its low strength as observed officially.

The standard charges of literature are

N	: **particle number,**
Q	: **electric charge,**
T	: **triality** *(1st strong component),*
L	: **lepton number.**

Actually, no forces are attributed to N and L. For the "strong" force, however, an additional, fictitious quantum number "*colour*" was invented (with values "red", "blue", and "green") so that a 3-quark baryon – contrary to Gell-Mann's original mixed-variant way of representation – could now officially be represented as formally "totally antisymmetric" with respect to its quark content, as well (Pauli's exclusion principle misunderstood by the SM).

Unofficially, this triplication of the number of "strong" forces is reproduced by the below quantum numbers A and M besides the above T – in a quite different mode of action, however: A is needed in nuclear physics in order to reproduce a certain mutual repulsion of nucleons; otherwise, a deuteron would not be interpreted as a compound of 2 nucleons but of 6 quarks. Correspondingly, M is needed for correctly reproducing the mass split in isospin multiplets.

Λ	: **leptonic charge,**
E	: **exotic charge,**
A	: **strong charge** *(2nd component),*
M	: **strong charge** *(3rd component).*

Λ is the weak monopole charge of "weak" interactions. E, then, is some still unknown, "exotic" charge we never mentioned before and for whose existence there is no evidence by experiment, yet, but which should nevertheless exist in New Physics for consistency considerations.

Now, a coupling *constant is* usually expected to be a "constant". Field theorists know that the coupling strength varies with squared energy-momentum, e.g. ("form factors"). Here again, the unitarity postulate of the reaction channel interferes with calculations made in the dynamic channel. In QG, those "form factors" are traced back to the non-valence part of a particle or to its "virtual tail".

Here, we distinguish between a coupling "constant" at some fixed value[s] of the form-factor argument – and the varying form factor itself. The quotient of that (gross) form factor over that (special) coupling constant is then the non-valence contribution to the coupling. Experimentalists are used to *extrapolating* their reaction yields towards those coupling *constants* by graphical methods.

For "strong" interactions, those *constant* parts are predominant, giving coupling constants of the order of 1 (in terms of mere "Clebsch-Gordon coefficients" respecting the valence contributions only). For gravity, those non-valence contributions prevail; their somewhat arbitrary normalisation is <u>defined</u> to be some invariant combination of customary measuring units giving rise to some rather tiny coupling value that mainly reflect some arbitrary position given by the non-valence part.

The most challenging case for mathematicians is the intermediate case like that we meet with "weak" interactions. On the one hand, that Yukawa-type potential form (arbitrarily assumed from solving the Klein-Gordon equation, which reflects just a *part* of QG) has to reflect the non-valence part of the exchange particle[s]. On the other hand, their exact structure made of quanta has actually not yet been ultimately identified by calculating it explicitly.

Nevertheless, the experimental comparison with tentative, preliminary results already tells us, that, due to its narrow central Yukawa peak with its correspondingly steep density gradient (!), the effective coupling <u>strength</u> of the "weak" intermediate <u>mono</u>-pole exchange particle should be much stronger than a corresponding coupling strength of "strong" interactions; the dipole exchange mesons W and Z offer some much too weak picture of the interaction!

<u>Only for readers interested in mathematics</u>, here is a hint about how we could learn some more details leading to the above initial, colourful table. Due to the lack of knowledge about its partition into space- and time-like dimensions, let us start organising its 8 combinations of the labels l, r, t in the reaction channel according to their sorting, as given in the left-hand column of that table. Depending on the generators G = L, M, P, Q of the 8 "internal" subgroups of the type U(2,2) commuting with each other, we find their relations to Dirac's extended a- and b-spins:

$G_\mu^{(0,+)}$	$G_\mu^{(1,-)}$	$G_\mu^{(2,-)}$	$G_\mu^{(3,-)}$	$G_\mu^{(1,+)}$	$G_\mu^{(2,+)}$	$G_\mu^{(3,+)}$	$G_\mu^{(0,-)}$
$a_{k111}^\pm$	$a_{k211}^\pm$	$a_{k121}^\pm$	$a_{k112}^\pm$	$a_{k122}^\pm$	$a_{k212}^\pm$	$a_{k221}^\pm$	$a_{k222}^\pm$
$b_{k111}^\mp$	$b_{k211}^\mp$	$b_{k121}^\mp$	$b_{k112}^\mp$	$b_{k122}^\mp$	$b_{k212}^\mp$	$b_{k221}^\mp$	$b_{k222}^\mp$

Their (symmetrical) conversion matrix U into the G collecting the 4 spin combinations (l',l"), (r',r"), (t',t") to Lorentz combinations 0, 1, 2, 3, now, reads:

$$\left(G_\mu^{(r,\pm)} \right) = U \left(G_{\mu\lambda\rho\tau} \right), \quad \left(G_{\mu\lambda\rho\tau} \right) = U \left(G_\mu^{(r,\pm)} \right),$$

$$U \equiv \tfrac{1}{\sqrt{8}} \begin{pmatrix} +1 & +1 & +1 & +1 & +1 & +1 & +1 & +1 \\ +1 & -1 & -1 & -1 & +1 & +1 & +1 & -1 \\ +1 & -1 & -1 & +1 & -1 & +1 & -1 & +1 \\ +1 & -1 & +1 & -1 & -1 & -1 & +1 & +1 \\ +1 & +1 & -1 & -1 & +1 & -1 & -1 & +1 \\ +1 & +1 & +1 & -1 & -1 & -1 & +1 & -1 \\ +1 & +1 & -1 & +1 & -1 & +1 & -1 & -1 \\ +1 & -1 & +1 & +1 & +1 & -1 & -1 & -1 \end{pmatrix}.$$

*For irreducibility (corresponding to the **quark confinement**), we still have to extract the trace singlet from U:*

$$G_{...,\lambda\rho\tau} = \left(G_{...,\lambda\rho\tau} - \tfrac{1}{3}\,\delta_{\lambda\rho\tau}\,G_{...,000}\right) + \tfrac{1}{3}\,\delta_{\lambda\rho\tau}\,G_{...,000},$$
$$\delta_{\lambda\rho\tau} \equiv (\delta_{\lambda0} + \delta_{\lambda3})(\delta_{\rho0} + \delta_{\rho3})(\delta_{\tau0} + \delta_{\tau3}).$$

(The extracted singlet will generate the ordinary QG.) Our initial colourful table, above, now results from adequate linear combinations of the above U-lines orthogonal to each other, in a way that looks plausible to us according to the experimental situation.)

QG defines this trace singlet by the quantum number N" of chapter 8. Up to its normalisation, N" will be equal to N within the quadrant before the event horizon after the big bang if N is positive. Only beyond this restriction, N" and N are different from each other. In so far, N" might be conditionally simulated by N, there.

As singlets, gravity and dark energy, each for itself carries the same sign within *all* parts of our universe. A sign change will occur only beyond its limits when an additional step towards another dimension doubling in a multiverse is introduced. Our actual singlet will then be extended to a doublet fitted with both signs (up and down), each. Thus, it will keep the individual universes at a distance within its compound.

31. The Chiral Forces of Nature

The table of Chapter 8 showing the 4x4 = 16 U(2,2)-generators may be transcribed for the chiral U(2,2) part starting with **electric charge Q** into the terms

Q	:	**electric charge**
B$_i$	:	**magnetic field** *(3 components)*
χ	:	**Lorentz gauge**
E$_i$	:	**electric field** *(3 components)*
A$_0$	:	(time-like) **electric potential**
A$_i$	:	(time-like) **magnetic potential** *(3 comp.)*
$\underline{A}_0$	:	(space-like) **electric potential**
$\underline{A}_i$	:	(space-like) **magnetic potential** *(3 comp.)*

In a suitable normalisation, they characterise the electromagnetic chiral part of the linear Casimir operator of charge Q together with its appropriate **electromagnetic SO(2,4) field tensor**

$F_{ab} = - F_{ba}$ with a,b ∈ {1,2,3,4,5,6} and μ,ν ∈ {1,2,3,5=0}:

F$_{\mu\nu}$	~ (B$_i$,E$_i$)	electromagnetic fields
F$_{46}$	~ χ	Lorentz gauge
F$_{\mu 6}$	~ A$_\mu$	electromagnetic 4-potential 1
F$_{\mu 4}$	~ $\underline{A}_\mu$	electromagnetic 6-potential 2

At least for those relatively weak fields we are familiar with on earth, the (*special*-relativistic, invariant) **Lorentz gauge** is usually set arbitrarily equal to zero because only its derivative enters the classical (special-relativistic) Maxwell equations. A and $\underline{A}$ represent the electromagnetic 4-potential in its time-like variant A (in analogy to linear momentum) and in its space-like variant $\underline{A}$ (in analogy to CMS-spacetime), respectively:

$$A_\mu A^\mu \geq 0,$$
$$\underline{A}_\mu \underline{A}^\mu \leq 0.$$

The classical case – Lorentz gauge = 0 – does not distinguish between A and A. As in the case of the ordinary singlet of QG, the alternative might be discussed here, too, if the one exchange particle – there the graviton, here the photon – should be replaced by an entire spectrum of particles, i.e., by _every_ state which, by its charge Q, might directly or indirectly contribute to the tensor F in 6 dimensions! *(The new problem, occurring here, would be the separation of the particle's contribution according to its Q-share to its total share of all 8 "internal" charge types.* In the previous chapter, we observed that every quantum carries several, different charges!*)*

Instead of limiting ourselves with gravity to the spin-2 graviton and with electrodynamics to the spin-1 photon, thus, all states would be at our disposal in order to exhaust the full variation width of the (6-dimensional) field tensor of the respective interaction type. This could settle the problem concerning the nucleons' magnetic moments.

For the triality component of strong interactions, there are completely analogous definitions, except that their range and **triality T** are characterised not by the Coulomb but by the Yukawa potential. This will result in extended field equations. Instead of introducing the dynamic tensor L or the electromagnetic tensor F, we shall have to insert into the

strong field tensor T_{ab} (to replace the L_{ab} or F_{ab}).

In the SM, strong interaction will still have to follow the colour logic valid there. As the counterpart of the one, massless photon of electrodynamics, the Lagrange formalism of chromodynamics artificially introduces a set of 8 massless vector bosons, called **gluons**, required to underlie that colour logic, there. Until now, however, those gluons avoided any direct observation. New Physics replaces the 3 colour variants of strong interactions by its 3 charges T, A, and M. The formal parametrisation, hence, should essentially be transferable.

With respect to weak interactions, the SM considers the 3 weak bosons W^+, W^-, and Z to represent its gauge bosons, i.e., there are 3 instead of the 1 boson due to gauge theory. Furthermore, gauge theory demands that its vector bosons are massless, in addition. Those weak bosons, however, are extremely massive! The SM tries to overcome this contradiction by applying its Higgs mechanism, which, by construction, is superfluous in QG: Mass, here, is a statistical property summing up directly from the individual quanta of the non-valence part of a particle.

*For the mathematicians: **Gauge theory**. By adding two of the 8 chiral components – say (000) and (333) (for, the same will hold true for the chiral singlet (000) of QG) – we obtain their combined quadratic Casimir*

$$C^{(2)}_{U(4,4)}(000) + C^{(2)}_{U(4,4)}(333) .$$

Let us pick out its terms of 4-momentum, G=P, and rename them

$$P_{\mu,000} \equiv \quad P_\mu ,$$
$$P_{\mu,333} \equiv -eA_\mu .$$

The result is

$$\left(P_0{}^2 - \vec{P}^2\right) + e^2\left(A_0{}^2 - \vec{A}^2\right)$$
$$= \frac{1}{2}\left((P_0 - eA_0)^2 - \left(\vec{P} - e\vec{A}\right)^2\right)$$
$$+ \frac{1}{2}\left((P_0 + eA_0)^2 - \left(\vec{P} + e\vec{A}\right)^2\right).$$

*With P as the 4-momentum of QG and A as the **electromagnetic 4-potential**, this is exactly the split according to the sign of the electromagnetic charge e familiar to us from the "**minimal coupling**" of electrodynamics:*

$$\textcolor{red}{P_\mu \ \to \ P_\mu \mp eA_\mu .}$$

*It is the classical result of a **gauge theory**, which can be extended to all chiral components. In addition to there, however, its embedment into the 2nd Casimir is implying total dynamics, masses included!*

32. The Geometry of Forces

Let me address a peculiarity with **particle number N** in the "internal" octet, which strongly resembles the linear Casimir – let us call it **N'** (see Chapter 8) of the "internal" singlet (i.e., of the original QG). Up to their coupling strengths and ranges, the difference between N and N' manifests itself just by a couple of signs. As already mentioned, that N logic has not yet been scrutinised in detail, however.

But let us remember the 4 quadrants with respect to the parities C and T (see Chapter 19). In the quadrant after the big bang on this side of the event horizon, we observe the original field tensors N and N'. In the black-red nesting sketch of Chapter 21, label k separates Dirac's spinor from his antispinor with respect to N, while the label pair (m,n) distinguishes Dirac's 4 components with respect to their U(2,2) pair in their explicit form U((1,1),(1,1)).

Within the same quadrant its quanta will thus repel each other (with respect to N") by **dark energy** as being "charged equally". This can be traced back to the negative **density gradient of entropy** – while the **attractive effect** is an **effect** resulting **from the deflection of an extended body within a layered medium**.

On the other side, however, from the geometrical point of view, rejection by dark energy is no more than the effect of a hyperbolic structure pointing outwards, while attraction by gravity is the effect of an elliptic structure pointing inwards. The limits of our universe, hence, will roughly result from the balance between both competing effects (and taking into account the thinning-out effect outwards).

For "internal" octet charges, those horizon limits are situated closer together in terms of effective particle radii. By this effect together with the considerably smaller number of quanta bound in the valence parts of ordinary matter than in our total universe bound in its dark matter, the repulsive power concentrated in our universe will be lowered from the scale of our universe to the atomic or even to subatomic orders of magnitude.

Contrary to that, the non-valence parts of particles and neutral particles, will rather behave like the effect of gluing putty. As an example, consider the neutrons keeping the atomic nucleus together – or the electrons keeping together the nuclei in matter.

33. Rejection and Attraction

QG can be traced back to individually conserved quantities, our quanta occurring in 8 different types. Their origin and the occupation numbers of their individual types are accepted as unknown to us: they are external parameters to the world we are living in. On principle, we could count them, but QG cannot predict them.

According to this embedment assumption, our world is organised in hierarchies (matryoshka principle). The hints towards a next lower GUT-level in terms of "internal" parameters are obvious; and another hint towards a next higher hierarchy is present in terms of an experimentally measured asymptotic flatness of our world in spite of its obvious curvature by Einstein's General Relativity and its dark energy behaviour is evident giving rise to multiverse speculations. We cannot prove it, but we might argue that these immediately neighbouring levels might be governed by the same physics which we are experiencing within our own level.

Our next lower level demonstrates by its quark confinement that it is $2**3 = 8$-dimensional, as well. Without a more profound experimental experience, however, we cannot predict how far this continuity of physical laws in the way we are familiar with will proceed. A preliminary result, however, seems to be nature's organisation in powers of 8 dimensions.

From GUT we know its quantum number N. On our side of the event horizon, after the big bang, that N might be proportional to the gravitational constant; but the U(4,4) belonging to that N is <u>not</u> <u>QG</u> because it switches the sign of its charge N when passing over to an antiparticle; QG does not do so. Hence, we are actually treating QG as a GUT-singlet. By a next-higher dimension doubling defining some multiverse our universe is a member of, this might be different!

There, our singlet "gravity" might be a component of some spinor whose additional component is charged oppositely with respect to gravity! Just remember the sign of heavy mass when passing the event horizon! Due to the entropic dark-energy effect, then, universes charged equally with respect to gravity would reject each other, while oppositely charged ones would attract each other.

This is like a hierarchy lower with the "internal" charges. Who could have imagined those different properties we met with the antiparticles before detecting them! There, we saw, oppositely charged "universes" preferentially are pairing to dark-matter structures like dark matter or non-valence parts. In the present case, this will give rise to what I have called a "salty universe", i.e., to some system of universes looking like a many-body solid state. This might characterise the nearest environment outside our own universe.

When, combining two neighbouring hierarchies of our 2nd-order world formula, there are not 8 but 8x8 = 64 dimensions: In addition, a dynamic octet times an "internal" octet relates oppositely charged components. Their equally charged components would have opposite signs with respect to their oppositely charged ones. Within that "internal" octet, however, it is unclear, actually, which of its components are space-like and which of them time-like. (Therefore, we are able to discuss this hierarchy level only in its reaction channel, at the moment.)

On the 2nd-order level of our world formula, this combination of 2 neighbouring hierarchies means the addition of all terms of the type noticed in the 2nd-order world formula for QG at the start of Chapter 10 – once for every one of the 8 dimensions of the other QG. (Hence, there will be a mechanical QG, an electromagnetic QG, etc.)

I just mentioned our actual uncertainty about which of the "internal" quantum numbers will have to be attributed to time-like and which of them to space-like dimensions in the dynamic channel. Those time-like "internal" contributions to the final world formula embracing both hierarchies, then, will not have to be added but subtracted. This attribution, hence, will have to be identified by experiment.

Dirac's interpretation of an **outgoing antiparticle as representing an incoming particle**, last but not least, has its logical but not its historical origin in the above partition of the total system according to

$$U(4,4) \supset U(2,2) \oplus U(2,2).$$

Here, one of the U(2,2)s multiplies the generators of the other U(2,2) by the imaginary unit. (Purely by group theory, a pair of generators, however, will represent 2 generators independent of each other. Hence, the dimension doubles from 4 to 8 in spinor space!) By the same logic, the doubling of gravity charge to a pair of positive and negative gravities, respectively, would start the next higher matryoshka cycle.

The same way as the 3 parities of our universe subdivide into those $2**3 = 8$ partial subareas, so does a quant with respect to its 8 "internal" charge components. None of these partial areas can survive on a stand-alone basis; by respecting certain rules (like the quark confinement, e.g.), they will have to join forces in order to build up some more sophisticated structure, i.e., a complete universe – corresponding to an elementary particle.

A quant, as an 8-vector, should therefore correspond to an 8-vector composed of partial-universe areas. Universes would thus have to be considered as tensor components made of adequate vector components. With particles, those 16 bricks of dark matter play some special role. The organisation of our own universe suggests some structure like them.

Such a construction of our universe, essentially as some neutral merger of two 8-vectors made of partial universal areas and being charged oppositely with respect to N, will become obvious, as well, by comparing the situation within our own universe (that part after the big bang on this side of the event horizon). Here, where we are able to measure, astronomers are verifying a huge surplus of dark over ordinary matter, which by QG, then, turns out even to be plausible. And ordinary matter, essentially, consists of neutral non-valence parts.

Provided that on both levels – universes and particles – we have the same axioms, indeed, then the most probable assumption would be: **Our universe** should be considered **as some brick corresponding to dark matter, only one level higher in hierarchy.** V.v., it follows that beyond the limitations of our own universe, we should even expect the presence of structures which are far more sophisticated (carrying valence parts). On that higher level, there should be structure corresponding to our own particles, as well, possibly even biological variants of life.

This way, the microscopic structure of our world might transfer to cosmic dimensions and v.v. As long as the axioms do not vary from level to level, **basic physics will stay the same**. Multiverses of the above provenience would melt into hyperuniverses of the type U((4,4),(4,4)), etc., until finding their end in a U((16,16),(16,16)).

With respect to fundamental forces, a wide discovery potential is still waiting for experimental physicists and astronomers! First of all, however, first pieces of evidence of interactions reaching beyond the limits of our own universe will still have to be identified. Purely by physics, overcoming such limits definitely is imaginable. The main obstacles, however, will be the **technical effort** to be spent.

Cosmic background radiation, with its levelling (flatness) of the general-relativistic curvature of space on the multiverse level, provided a first, promising, experimental data record in this direction, already; cf. Chapter 27. The crucial difference to the bubble model of eternal inflation is that, in QG, those "bubbles" are well-structured (according to Young tableaux).

Here, rejection and attraction, respectively, are expressed by the **charge sign** within an octet. Opposed to that is the opposite behavioural pattern of uncorrelated dark-matter structures where we observe the additional gravity effect of extended structures converting their power just into the opposite direction, as well. Due to actual knowledge, the two effects are independent of each other.

34. Leptons

Due to the much smaller "weak" *mono*-pole horizon (not to be confounded with the much broader *di*-pole width of the "weak" bosons),
the "blue" isospin components of the colourful table of Chapter 30
will couple much stronger to each other than 2 "strongly" interact-
ing yellow or green quanta are doing:

$$H_Q \gg H_G \gg H_T \gg H_\Lambda .$$

The gravity horizon (2nd from the left) is given by the (asymptotic)
size of our universe. (By cosmic expansion, spacetime will increase
with time on the expense of energy-momentum.) By the form-factor
method mentioned already, the Yukawa mass of the graviton will
turn out to be extremely small.

The electromagnetic horizon (in the extreme left) is that large
only because the photon mass is vanishing. All massive (intermediate) particles will have a much smaller horizon. And, because there
will be many more particles carrying a triality force than a Λ force,
the triality horizon will be considerably larger than the Λ-horizon. A
"blue" quant, therefore, will predominantly couple to another "blue"
quant carrying the opposite Λ-charge.

Such a quantum pair, neutral with respect to Λ, is called an

anti-leptonucleus: $a^+_{\bar{r},212} a^+_{\bar{r},112}$.

leptonucleus: $b^+_{\bar{r},212} b^+_{\bar{r},112}$

In order to saturate its triality charge, in addition, a "green" quant
will still have to be multiplied. Depending on which of the 2 "green"
quanta at our disposal we choose, the total electric charge will be
either +1 or zero. We call it an electrically charged **antilepton** and

its **antineutrino**. Leptons, therefore, are antibaryons and antileptons are baryons.

Depending on the symmetry type, we obtain 3 lepton "generations":

- an antisymmetrical **electron** family,
- a mixed-symmetrical **muon** family,
- and a symmetrical **tauon** family.

Lepton flavours, hence, are nothing other than symmetry properties. The "standard" model does not know this because it treats leptons as "point particles" having no intrinsic structure. A more detailed, less rough consideration, however, will reveal a more sophisticated substructure (cf. at the end of this chapter).

Now, the quantum number Q is responsible for atomic spectra and chemistry; it fixes the size of an atom. Triality T fixes the size of a nucleus, Λ the size of a leptonucleus. Let us compare the structure of a deuterium atom with that of an electron:

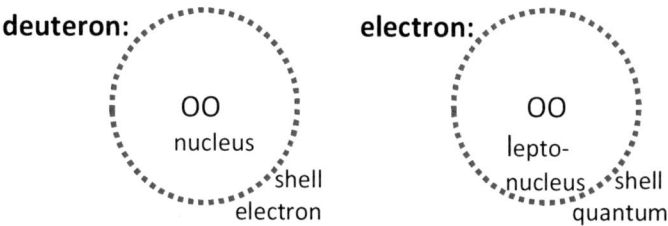

The structure is the same – with the different force types, however, their scales differ by orders of magnitude. When the "standard" model treats an **electron as a "point particle"**, this means that it is treating leptons in a way elder physicists once treated atoms before Rutherford proved that they carry a nucleus inside. With leptons, hence, theory is still actually in the times before Rutherford.

With the above sketch of an electron, we are in the fortunate situation that we can explicitly calculate the **fine-structure constant**, that legendary value of 1/137.036 because the photon mass is vanishing. With a photon energy tending to zero, the non-valence parts of the input and output electron are then equal and therefore will drop out.

Due to the extraordinary importance of this calculation, as an exception, let us notice its details. The reader who is not interested in them should simply skip the following explanations before arriving at the final result. *Details:*

We are familiar with the effect that we cannot walk through a massive wall made of concrete. Although this wall is electrically neutral as a whole, the negative charges of the electron shells of its atoms prevent us from penetrating it because the equally negative charges of the electron shells we are carrying in us reject them. For the same reason we do not fall through the floor.

Conclusion: We shall have to properly distinguish between the total charge of some compound and the partial charges of its constituents! In classical physics, this distinction, <u>by definition</u> (!), should not make any difference for an electron because there the electron is assumed to be a point particle.

In the GUT, however, an electron – comparable to a deuterium atom – will consist of 3 constituents: a leptonucleus tightly binding 2 quanta together, around which a third quantum is "circling" which is bound much less strongly. In a low-energy approach according to the "method wall", we predominantly will "feel" that shell quantum, but not yet the pair in the nucleus.

To calculate the fine-structure constant, hence, we first obtain the squared electric charge −2/3 of that third quantum as a factor. It is to be multiplied by the true coupling constant (which is the squared "Clebsch-Gordon coefficient" of the coupling). Particle physicists calculate it as the "expectation value" (a matrix) of the photon sandwiched between the 2 spinor components of the electron, which, in the case of forward scattering, are equal.

In the easiest case, the valence part of a photon is composed of 2 quanta. In an operator description, we could approach it by a generator. Irreducibility of this 2-quant representation, then, requires tearing out its trace. This gives rise to a factor:

$$1 - \frac{1}{64} = \frac{63}{64}.$$

After the separation of dark matter, only 60 of the original 64 dimensions of the electron representation (diminished by the leptonucleus) are left. Our photon state acts on 1 of them: factor 1/60. By collecting terms, the fine-structure constant, neglecting its dipole contributions originating from its leptonucleus, turns out simply to be

$$\alpha = \left(-\frac{2}{3}\right)^2 \cdot \frac{63}{64} \cdot \frac{1}{60} = \frac{1}{137.143}.$$

When compared with the experimental value 1/137,036, our lowest-order approximation, already has a precision of

$$\frac{\alpha_{\text{theor.}} - \alpha_{\text{exp.}}}{\alpha_{\text{exp.}}} \approx 0.08\,\%.$$

For more complex valence structures like those in a proton or neutron, where 3 similar valence quanta have to share the cake, this classical result for the **electron as a point particle** will have to be fitted with additional contributions. This becomes obvious with their magnetic momenta.

(As in the balance of reversible against irreversible time, here again, the replacement of the photon represented by means of a generator coupling an input with an output quantum gives rise to form factors. (A photon valence in the input will be added to the non-valence part in the output.) In the limit of vanishing photon energy, however, those deviations will converge towards 1.

In literature, transitions via still different intermediate states than the photon, by definition (!), often are not attributed to electromagnetism but shifted over to additional interactions that we do not control as well. This is idealising and simplifying the calculation of "pure" quantum electrodynamics tremendously.)

As in the case of the electromagnetic pair E and B of forces derived from the electromagnetic 4-potential A, there should be derived pairs of forces from the "strong" and "weak" interactions obeying "strong" and "weak" "Maxwell equations", respectively, too. Only, the question arises of how large are the respective rest masses of their corresponding "strong" and "weak" "photons", how strong are their effective couplings, and how long are their ranges.

In addition, it is by no means clear if those corresponding states of minimal rest masses each carries a spin =1 like the photon, a spin =2, like the graviton, or whatever spin. Remember that every individual quantum represents some *mixture* of diverse "internal" charges. When literature postulates that those "carriers" of an interaction all should have a spin =1, then, this is a result of **gauge theory**. Our model, however, is Quantum Gravity!

This calculation of the fine-structure constant immediately points to the correctness of a multitude of assumptions typical for QG:

- A lepton is not a point particle but a composed structure.
- The leptonucleus consists of quanta different to those of the hadrons, fitted with a much stronger binding power.
- The basic dimension of our GUT is 8x8 = 64, indeed.
- 4 of the 64 types of quanta are snatched away completely, as requested by dark matter.

Only for people interested in mathematics, let us specify the 3 lepton flavours already detected in more detail, here. Additional ones should still have considerably higher masses and should thus be far less stable. According to Chapter 41, their "neutrinos" should be massive.

In their decomposition chain of our U(32,32), here, their subgroup U(8)xSU(2) is relevant. Dirac's 8 ordinary b-spins would be equal for all 3 generations, i.e.,S = 1/2; but the "internal" symmetry configurations of their 3-quant valences are differing:

	U(16)	U(8)$_{\text{"internal"}}$	SU(2)$_{\text{spin}}$
e^-, ν_e	totally symmetrical	mixed symmetrical	mixed symmetrical
μ^-, ν_μ	mixed symmetrical	mixed symmetrical	mixed symmetrical
τ^-, ν_τ	totally symmetrical	anti symmetrical	mixed symmetrical

35. Excited States

An irreducible particle state is defined by some adequate Young frames. In our 8x8 = 64 dimensions, such an irreducible Young tableau is an array of 64 rows at most. The number of its columns is limited by the total number of its quanta, which, in QG, is assumed to be great when compared with the number 64 of rows, because it has to be subject to the macroscopic law of great numbers.

The most probable configuration of its **non-valence part**, hence, will be the totally symmetrical one consisting of 1 single row. We choose it as our first-order starting approximation. *(Extensions could develop to applications of Wigner's "Random Matrices".)* A non-valence part is analysed according to its decomposition according to certain subgroups as suggested by the colourful table of the chapter "Charges". There will be plenty of "yellow" pair components, plenty of "green" ones, considerably fewer "blue" ones, and still fewer "red" ones – this is the assumption, at all.

In a lowest-order approximation, all these components multiply each other. This fits our statement that a particle should be understood as some locally constructive superposition of components of our irreducible universe. We observed, already, that – contrary to the dark-matter case – our "coloured" non-valence components do *not* sum their "internal" labels (with the exception of a few dark-matter bricks accidentally having been mixed in, here).

Our Chapter 30 only shows the (jk)-values (a,+) at the left-hand rim of its table. The remaining Dirac components entering dark matter may be added correspondingly. In dark matter, there are 4x4 = 16 types of paired Dirac spinors; their spin labels (i',i") have been left open, there. Shortly after Gell-Mann's presentation of his quark model, people still supplemented "**S-, P-, D-waves**" etc., which should represent supposed **orbital angular momenta**, into his quark model in order to reproduce additional types of particle resonances not yet covered by Gell-Mann's first quark ansatz.

S-waves (orbital angular momentum =0) correspond to Gell-Mann's original quark model. P-waves (orbital angular momentum =1) transform Gell-Mann's pseudo-scalar mesons (spin, parity) = (0,−) to "axial-vector mesons" with (spin, parity) = (1,+), or his ordinary vector mesons (1,−) to ordinary scalar mesons (0,+), i.e., to particles carrying the opposite parity, each.

Above all, however, these higher-wave states enabled a **quick increase of spin values** for particles that otherwise, would have to stay at the low orders of magnitude their isospin values are offering.

This is one of the reasons that encouraged people to take that historically fatale short-cut postulate that particles should be composed of no more than 3 quarks (baryons) or of 1-quark-1-antiquark pairs (mesons). As a result, people had to artificially separate leptons from hadrons. Many, important mesons (like the "weak" bosons, e.g.), had no place within the "standard" model. Endless fights with and against "symmetry breaking" started without any need, etc., etc.

Perhaps one of the most serious problems still present nowadays was created by barring the path towards a successful construction of Quantum Gravity with its non-valence parts – a scientific disaster of the first order that can be traced back to Gell-Mann's times.

The truth, however, is that those "orbital" angular momenta, having been attached to the particle's valence part, are (Q=1)-multiplets of CMS-location Q, e.g., which were shoveled from the non-valence to the valence part in order, formally, to satisfy an unrequested conservation property with respect to some stand-alone valence part. On the other hand, a particle's valence part *is* no self-consistent property in group theory: Just the *combination* of a valence with a non-valence part is requested to be irreducible in toto, at most! – Usually, all those details are of no special relevance. For "weak" interactions, however, they acquired historical significance (as parity "breaking", e.g.).

Translated into Dirac's 4-dimensional spinor mathematics, the non-valence part of a particle is something like a superposition of products of powers of the 16 dark-matter components discussed in Chapter 26. Their summation over the "internal" labels, however, is suspended, and the summed dark-matter components are dropped.

Their components a^+b^+, a^+a^-, b^+b^-, a^-b^-, there, when combined to an S-wave (spin=0), thus, correspond to the U(2,2)-generators L_0 (linear Casimir), P_0 (energy), Q_0 (CMS-time), and M_0 (heavy mass), but separately for all the colours "yellow", "green", "blue", and "red" in the Chapter 30.

P-waves will be added by those analogues to the corresponding spin=1 combinations L_i (spin), P_i (linear momentum), Q_i (CMS-location), and M_i (Lorentz-boost). Higher waves are represented as powers of these P-waves.

The corresponding states, now, allow for a diagonalisation with respect to 4 generators, each – say L_0, P_0, Q_3, and L_3 – belonging to all 2x4 "colourful" chiral components involved ("iso-up" and "iso-down", each in "yellow", "green", "blue", and "red"). The application of the related generators will yield some list of partial counts, whose summation over all colours we shall have to interpret as particle number, energy, CMS-location (3-direction), and spin (same direction).

By construction, particle number N (see Chapter 31) will be very small because, here, it will depend on the valence part only. Provided we want to give macroscopic statements like those concerning Einstein's spacetime, we cannot avoid applying the law of great numbers because heavy mass is not simultaneously commensurable.

Similar problems will arise if we want simultaneously to give results on all 3 directions and/or on linear momentum, in addition, or even on time.

With respect to a valence part, a P-wave state represents some "**excitation**" of the original S-wave state. An S-wave, here, is an excitation of order zero. Neglecting singlet representations is almost a principle in conventional field theories. This is the source of those classical excesses when relating the electromagnetic interaction to chiral components by means of that "**minimal coupling**" looking so curious from the group-theoretical perspective or – to quote another example – of those intellectual acrobatics done about the subject "Higgs".

In field theories, those basic "zeroth orders" are hardly considered. In QG, however, they significantly determine the **rest mass** of a particle, i.e., they are no mere attachments to annoy the reader! From the perspective of QG, the **Higgs model is superfluous**: particle mass is simply generated by summing up all S-wave contributions in its rest system. Instead, mass<u>less</u> particles are the exception – to be massive is standard.

The value of a respective rest mass is given by the quadratic world formula. The problem is only the explicit value of its Casimir <u>constant</u>, which is a function of the creation history of our world where the 64 total occupation numbers of each quantum type had been fixed from outside. The rest mass within our time slice in our actual universe, then, is a matter of probability: The rest mass is the most probable expectation value of the special particle constellation in question, related to all other competing particles and, then, fixed by Bell's superdeterminism.

By varying the individual parameters within the world formula, its mass value is varied, too. But contrary to the traditional field theories having some fixed rest mass, those **"virtual" mass values** belong to the irreducible representation of a particle as integral parts – so to speak, as some "tail" term that does not need to be generated by Feynman's special Fourier method in addition: It is simply present from the start.

36. Shell Models

The valence part of a hydrogen molecule is composed of that of a proton (as a baryon) and that of an electron (as an antibaryon). As separate particles, the proton and the electron will both have their own non-valence parts, as well. As a compound hydrogen state, however, they will have just one common non-valence part.

External P-wave excitations, then, will enlarge that common non-valence part step by step, modifying it by unevenly building up individual substructures around the 2 valence parts until they finally allow for decomposition of these 2 partial substructures. In the end, each of them will separately carry its own individual, complete, independent non-valence part in terms of a "free" electron and a "free" proton, respectively.

Let us track such a liberation process from the perspective of the electron's valence part. The external P-waves – taken over from a colliding photon, e.g. – will multiply the "S-wave ocean" already present in the hydrogen compound. If – according to the previous chapter – we take it for granted that a particle state most probably should be represented symmetrically, those additional P-waves (made of 2 quanta, each) will line up to a single Young row. For a 3-fold excitation, this is schematically:

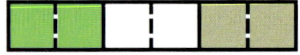

Every (pseudo-)unitary Young box will represent a spin = 1/2 each. 2 components ("up" and "down", a double box) hence will hence give a combination of spin 1 and spin 0, i.e., of 3+1 = 4 = 2x2 individual components. The above symmetrical Young line made of 3 double boxes, thus, describes a spin=3 state (spins 1+1+1), a spin=2 state (spins 1+1+0 = 1+0+1 = 0+1+1), a spin=1 state (spins 1+0+0 = 0+1+0 = 0+0+1), and a spin=0 state (0+0+0). That far mathematics will take us.

Atomic physicists, however, agreed to a somewhat different notation: They singled out the above 2 "green" boxes by assigning them to the electron spin and to the proton spin, respectively. Only the remaining double boxes, then, are designated to represent an "orbital momentum". Atomic physicists call that number of double boxes (above: 3) its "**principal quantum number**". Such a principal quantum number p, hence, will contain p electron "**shells**" carrying spins $I = 0, 1, 2, \ldots, p-1$, respectively. Every spin I has $2i+1$ components running from $-i, -i+1, \ldots, +i-2, +i-1, +i$. This is the "**shell model**" of atomic physics that gives rise to the **periodic system** of chemistry as we know it from school.

The "green" quantum has its origin in the coloured $8\times8 = 64$-dimensional representation of quanta in Chapter 30. If we, again, assume the totally symmetric Young representations as their most probable cases (in 64 dimensions) for the valence parts of the electron and the proton, we obtain a single Young row made of 3 quanta, each, with labels running independently of each other from 1 to 64 in both cases. Especially for an electron or positron, 2 of these quanta are to be chosen as "blue" ones and 1 as a "green" one, while, for a proton or antiproton, the 2 "blue" ones are to be replaced by "yellow ones:

The decomposition of such a 64-dimensional 3-quant representation into a product of two 8-dimensional representations – one for QG, another one for the "internal" labels – will yield that mixed-symmetric baryon representation of spin 1/2 well known from Gell-Mann (and his totally symmetric representation of baryon resonances carrying spin 3/2), plus additional representations that are not of interest, here.

For the above left-hand Young pattern, this is the representation of an electron, e.g., and for the right-hand Young pattern that of a proton. By multiplying both valence parts, we finally obtain the "green" double-quant excitation of order zero (i.e., the actual spins of the proton and electron) treated at the beginning of this chapter.

Now, apart from their opposite particle numbers, the difference between an electron and a proton is the substitution of "blue" against "yellow" quanta. *In principle* both systems thus differ from each other only in external formalities, only. A system made of protons will hence behave basically in the same way as a system made of electrons will do. This is the "**shell model of nuclear physics**".

The number of protons that – after having been summed over shells filled before already – complete one of their own shells, in nuclear physics are called "**magic numbers**". Now, in atomic physics and in nuclear physics, the higher shells will not necessarily be filled up in the same order. For higher values, hence, the magic numbers may differ from each other for higher values within both realms of application.

Distinctions between the two shell models will arise from their behaviour towards their isospin partners, in addition: Neutrinos are massless; hence, they will quickly evaporate into neighbouring space, while neutrons – being of comparable sizes as protons – will become effective as "putty" among the protons, which reject each other electrically. Beside the "shell model of protons" they will add another "shell model of neutrons".

In addition, the (effective) magic numbers of the shell model of neutrons will differ slightly from the shell model of protons. The reason that interactions among the nucleons, due to their differing charges, will not proceed exactly in the same way. Apart from such an unbalance in their filling order, all shell models are identical.

37. Flavours

The **particle number N** (Chapter 30) or N' (Chapter 32) separates mesons (N=0) from baryons (N=+1), antibaryons (N=−1), and the "rest" (nuclei, atoms, molecules, fluids, solid states, …). In comparison, those 4 colours, "yellow", "green", "blue", and "red", separate 4 types of "**flavours**" from each other.

Gell-Mann's "**hadrons**", by definition, are composed of "yellow" and/or "green" quanta only: mesons of 2 quanta of opposite particle number N, baryons and antibaryons of 3 quanta carrying equal particle numbers N, each. The „Standard" Model (SM) is arbitrarily prohibiting a "hadron" from being composed of more than those 2 or 3 quanta, each. This permuted to the logical source of "flavour" physics.

A 5-quant baryon will therefore have to be represented by 3 quanta only, e.g. The 2 remaining quanta will secretly have to hide behind one of the other 3 quanta. Therefore, the SM is hiding its 2 "blue" quanta representing the leptonucleus behind its "green" quantum. The resulting 3-quant compound "green-blue-blue", then, is called a "lepton" which, by definition, will have to be some non-hadronic "point particle" without any substructure.

This, of course, only will work as long as the substructure of a lepton is not revealed. Now, our calculation of the fine-structure constant in comparison with its experimental value uniquely demonstrates the existence of that substructure. This disproves the ansatz made by the SM.

By their **leptonic flavours** (electron, muon, tauon systems), leptons, like baryons, are 3-quant states whose hidden ("blue") pair of quanta is carrying _equal particle numbers_. The **hadronic flavours**, however, are 5-quant states, instead, composed of a ("yellow-yellow-green") 3-quant nucleon and a ("green") 2-quant meson whose hidden ("green") 2-quant pair is carrying _opposite particle numbers_.

Leptonic flavours are therefore characterized by quantum pairs of equal particle numbers, hadronic flavours by quantum pairs of opposite particle numbers. In addition, both flavour types disagree in the construction of their names: Leptonic flavour pairs carrying different electric charges Q have the same flavour name (muon, muon-neutrino, e.g.), hadronic flavour pairs, however, have different names according to their electric charges: **"Charm" and "strangeness"** characterise the same ("green") flavour level, e.g., while **"top" and "bottom"** belong to an additional ("yellow") flavour level.

For hadronic flavours, there is still another restriction whose origin is from history: Its 3-quant compound of a single quant carrying that additional meson "rucksack" has to build up an overall spin=1/2 complex in order that this flavoured 3-quant complex will become *formally* compatible with to the unflavoured single quanta.

Now, in QG parities are generated by its generators. Hence, there is **1 common parity definition** for all states. In the "Standard" model, there is no such common definition: Instead, there are several independent definitions in parallel, depending on the individual particle families. Parity definitions, hence, differ from each other in QG and in the SM.

In QG, space-inversion parity is thus opposite for nucleons and leptons, e.g., because leptons, here, have been identified as antibaryons. Similar results will hold for the other flavours: As a 2-quant meson has negative parity, a simple-flavoured baryon or meson, due to its "rucksack", has the opposite parity as their unflavoured counterparts.

Corresponding contradictions arise with isospin assignments. In QG, all 8x8 = 64 quantum types equally carry isospin – even the leptons. In QG, hence, there are **no "symmetry breakings"**, while the SM is full of them. The SM solemnly celebrates its "breaking rules", even connecting isospin violations with hypercharge properties – a bizarre situation from the QG-point of view!

In QG, all those particle reactions proceed totally free of violations, even with "weak" interactions – no matter whether leptonic or non-leptonic. When a flavoured particle sheds its rucksack (decay into its unflavoured particle plus a meson), the SM, due to its inconsistent definitions of isospin and parities, will interpret that as some case of "symmetry breaking" to be handled by sophisticated breaking rules, while for this standard case in QG nobody will observe any reason to worry about it.

A special case is the excitation of the pion isospin triplet together with its isospin-zero singlet (the eta-meson). QG keeps that triplet + singlet structure:

$$(\pi^+, \pi^0, \pi^-) + \eta \implies (K^+, K_{long}, K^-) + K_{short}.$$

In the SM, this will yield the 2 kaon doublets contragredient to each other, instead, which result (as superpositions) directly from "strong" interactions. From the experiment, however, we know that the neutral kaons will have to be interpreted in the pattern sketched above. With the "green" rucksack above replaced by a "yellow" one, we are getting the respective heavier D-mesons, instead.

For the quartet of spin-3/2 baryon resonances we observe the special case that only 3 of them contain (at least) 1 isodown quant. Out of the isoquartet of the 4 Δ-resonances without strangeness, the first excitation level of one of its isodown quanta, hence, will give no Σ quartet but, according to spin, just a Σ (or Σ^*) triplet. By analogy, we find a Σ_c triplet by exciting its iso-up quant, instead. By replacing all 3 isodown quanta inside the baryon resonance Δ^-, we, finally, obtain the Ω^-. Intermediate steps are the Ξ-resonances.

The "weak" **W- and Z-mesons** are to be interpreted as bosons containing both, a leptonucleus and an anti-leptonucleus, simultaneously side by side. Together with 2 "green" quanta, they thus consist of at least 2x3 = 6 quanta, each.

It would be boring to continue with "green" or "yellow" hadronic flavours. The standard particles also might be interpreted as "green" or "yellow" leptonic flavours. "Blue"-and "red"-type *hadronic* flavours have not yet been a matter of inspection.

Finally, let us mention that the particular isospin component of the flavour "rucksack" (isoup-isoup, isodown-isodown) will have no essential effect on the hadronic flavour result: K- and D-mesons do not distinguish each other by their iso-component but by their isospin flavour ("green", "yellow"). We arrive at this conclusion by the smallness of the particles' mass split within an isomultiplet. If at all, it could be quadratic isospin (isosinglet vs. isotriplet) that could give rise to some slight variation in the particle spectrum. Statistically, however, this is expected to get lost in the resonance widths as some "washed-out" double peak. (The especially light pion-eta pair is an exception; for, the mass split is no linear effect.)

38. Pauli's Exclusion Principle

Pauli's exclusion principle has its origin in atomic physics, i.e., in the order of electrons in an atomic shell. Its statement is that, there, no 2 electrons are allowed to occupy the mathematically identical quantum state: Exactly equal states, hence, do not bind each other but must reject each other. This property, then, has successfully been taken over to nuclear physics.

It was left to the particle physicists arbitrarily to restrict this principle in a way to postulate 2 "equal" fermions that behave totally antisymmetrically to each other, instead. This postulate by the 1940 "spin-statistics theorem" might be sufficient – but it is not necessary: People have been going on playing those old careless and unjustifiable games according to which quantum field theories are used to work from their start on. It is not amusing any more.

Fact is that Young tableaux are limited in the number of antisymmetric entries by the dimension of their basic transformation group. In our U(64) or U(32,32) case this is 64. More than that relatively small number of particles cannot become totally antisymmetrised within an irreducible framework; hence, the opposite claim by the old spin-statistics theorem cannot be true! For symmetric entries, however, there is no such limit.

The (according to Bell's superdeterminism) "macro"-scopic argument of the 1940 spin-statistics theorem in favour of that antisymmetry postulate is founded on semi-classical comparisons of angular directions whose basic spacetime generators – as in the case of that putative "breakdown" of the wave function in a measuring process – are not even microscopically commensurable. As a result, Pauli's exclusion principle will actually have to be considered as some merely experimental fact without a theoretically founded proof.

On the other hand, Pauli's principle quite simply follows from the experimental split of our 64 dimensions into the 8 dimensions of QG times those 8 "internal" dimensions. "Equal" particles coinciding in their "internal" quantum numbers hence reject each other the closer they come. Quantum-theoretically, then, wave functions should not overlap too strongly; otherwise, they would run the risk of being torn to pieces by that powerful mutual rejection.

This, by the way, does not apply only to fermions but to bosons as well. There, only, the *absence* of too strong monopole forces is usually either tacitly assumed or they represent "internal" *singlet* states. ("Equal" *"internal" singlet* forces are *attractive*, cf. gravity.)

39. The Spectrum of Stable Particles

A Young frame with maximally 64 rows also should address a minimum of 64 stable particle states into which unstable states could decay or be decomposed by thermodynamic collision processes. As in our world everything is connected with everything (irreducibility property), the count of its basic components will proceed with some difficulty – except we are staying with the original quanta. Examples of those problems will immediately arise from the life times of special radioactive elements, whose half-life periods quite possibly might be longer than the age of our earth.

Particular components of this level certainly are those 16 dark-matter states and the 16 = 2x8 states of the proton-antiproton and of the electron-positron systems (carrying 2 spin components, each, 2 energy signs, and 2 signs designating particle number: 2**3 = 8). More problematic will be the additional 16 = (3+1)*2*2 + 1*2*2 neutrino plus **photon** states. Their helicities replacing spin distribute themselves fifty-fifty on particles and on antiparticles.

Quite generally, neutrinos – of whichever type – due to their odd particle number are principally massive. On the other hand, their rest masses are so tiny (macroscopically vanishing) that there should be some continuous, virtual fluctuation between positive and negative values. The SM, therefore, proposed some rather sophisticated decay mechanism in order to describe the transition ("**neutrino-oscillation**") among the 3 "blue" neutrino types experimentally observed.

QG offers a more pragmatic solution: With that small transition rate observed it would fully suffice to replace that complicated *decay* mechanism of the SM by some **collision** process where a neutrino is hit by a dark-matter brick thus unconventionally triggering the neutrino to switch over from one symmetry (flavour) type to another one. This procedure would not need those conventional statements about individual neutrino masses that are hard to check.

If we thus continue to consider neutrinos as macroscopically massless *on this intermediate level*, then, to complete our **system of stable particle states**, there are still 64–3x16 = 16 stable particle states not yet identified. Without any doubt, structures containing "blue" and, first of all, "red" quanta will be part of them, none of which, actually, is yet known to us. However, I do not want to speculate; here, experiment is requested.

40. The Parity Problem of Neutrinos

Massless states are the ideal partners to pass the event horizon of a black hole. Possibly there is a connection not yet uncovered between the **masslessness** of certain particles and their **parity "horizons"** within our universe.

Quite generally, that classical "**parity violation**" of nuclear beta-decay, by the way, **is "fake news"** because parities are fixed for particles at rest. Neutrinos, however, move with the speed of light. The point, now, is that energy-momentum is not commeasurable with the Lorentz-boost!

The Lorentz-acceleration of a particle at rest towards the speed of light, purely by mathematics, will yield a fifty-fifty parity mixture. And this is exactly what experiment verifies with the neutrinos. The reason that conventional theory has not yet accepted this trivial connection is that parity (as a discrete "label" of the valence part) is handled separately from energy-momentum (as a continuous "argument" of the non-valence part). "Irreducibility", however, will mix the valence with its non-valence part in a unique way; there is no place for a "violation" of parity.

The real problem behind it is that a neutrino is observed in one and the same helicity state, always, while the opposite helicity is reserved to its antineutrino. This **helicity split** between a particle and its antiparticle is a unique behaviour in physics, indeed. But its logic origin has nothing to do with a "violation" of parity! In QG, this helicity split quite simply is a result of the world formula in its third order applied to a macroscopically massless fermion. Its leading term reads:

$$C^{(3)}_{SU(2,2)} \propto \left(\vec{\tilde{L}} \cdot \vec{\tilde{M}} \right) M_0 + \ldots = \text{const.}$$

L here represents total angular momentum (spin + orbit), M its corresponding total boost, and M_0 heavy mass.

Hence, the bracket just projects particle spin onto its running direction. As a fermion, the particle, in any case, will have some mass that, microscopically, does not vanish. Last but not least, this, together with the constant value of the Casimir, will fix the sign of the bracket, i.e., its **helicity**. With a spin shift, then, either the mass (particle-antiparticle exchange) or the running direction automatically will change its sign, too.

Exactly this rigid **triangle relation** among spin (**helicity**), running **direction**, and **particle nature** is observed experimentally! Thus, for the first time, that **defective neutrino behaviour** is completely explained by theory; it is achieved on behalf of QG.

What theory, actually, does not yet explain is the complete spectrum of stable particles (cf. the preceding chapter). By theory, this specification would be a matter of numerical trial and error to be applied to corresponding test configurations of non-valence parts whose task it would be to reproduce the experimental resonance structure better and better.

41. Masslessness

In traditional particle physics, "resonances" are real particles; in QG, however, only those 64 absolutely stable states rank among them. In addition to its 8 "internal" octets, ToE still supplements the "internal" trace singlet, i.e., QG, together with the corresponding trace singlet of dynamics, while the double trace singlet "1", due to the irreducibility of ToE, should be dropped:

$$64_{ToE} - 1_{ToE\text{-}trace} \supset$$
$$8x8_{chiral\ octets} + 8x1_{QG} + 1x8_{dynamic\ singlet}.$$

Particle physics distinguishes between pure dynamics (GG) and its **material basis** (GUT) to which it has to be applied. The "dynamical singlet" will serve only for transforming those 8 chiral octets into each other, thus representing just another, more abstract form of dynamics we did not yet treat in detail.

By separating those two 8-dimensional singlets (8x1 + 1x8) from their material basis 8x8, we are losing 8+8 = 16 material states, which we shall have to omit when adding those 16 = 4x4 dark-matter components to the material basis.

In physics, this omission could be achieved by reducing those 3 neutrinos and the photon from 8 to just 4 components, each (helicity and the energy sign), e.g. This might explain why those four particles, in the consistency sense of Bell's superdeterminism, present themselves as massless, indeed. Its implementation, then, will proceed by the third-order world formula, as described in the preceding chapter.

42. Resonances

Chapter 10 ended with the singularity of the classical "propagator". To circumvent this singularity, Feynman's logic artificially admitts some tiny imaginary part to heavy mass. The propagator will thus will assume the form of a bell-shaped curve having some finite **peak** replacing the singularity, and the imaginary part will yield the **width of the peak**.

In QG, this bell-shaped curve is the result of a (macroscopic) probability (amplitude) responsible for a virtual state depending on energy and linear momentum; its value, hence, will at most be equal to 1.

Feynman once organised the **diagrams,** which should represent his particle reactions graphically, in terms of some network being constructed out of 3-legged **vertices**, the outcoming leg of one vertex having to be identified with an ingoing leg of some neighbouring vertex, with the connecting line of both vertices representing the propagator. States with one open end not ending at a vertex, then, represent incoming and outgoing stable particles:

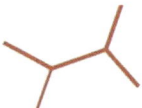

By the variation of propagators, however, plenty of singularities pile up to be argued away by much-needed persuasion (keyword: **"renormalisation"**: infinite minus infinite giving finite!).

On the other hand, QG works with probabilities in the reaction channel, hence everything will stay finite. The propagators represent virtual states. As **"resonances"**, they collectively reflect the additional quanta characterising the other two lines of a vertex. The resonance resulting from 2 stable states typically yield some kind of a bell-shaped curve with a peak of some width the properties of which might be derived from those of the two stable states of the vertex.

Technically, this task should be mastered numerically (on a computer). Feynman needed that network in order to calculate the final state. QG, on the other hand, proceeds the inverse way by using the starting and final states to determine dominant intermediate states.

(On a next higher level above the quanta) QG is based on a material basis of 64 stable representations replacing those 64 types of quanta one level lower. On this higher level, all additional matter will secondarily be composed of them. Which are those 64 representations is a matter of Bell's superdeterminism responsible for the consistency of the entire construction.

43. Numbers and Quanta

Vectors in n dimensions add up n objects e ("**dimensions**") that are independent of each other. By definition, a vector allows multiplication with numbers. In physics, those numbers are usually either r- or c-numbers:

$$V = a_1\vec{e}_1 + \ldots + a_n\vec{e}_n.$$

Actually, the multiplication of such "objects" should be irrelevant because **QG is mere tensor arithmetic** applying Kronecker products only, i.e., multiple vectors not modifying those objects. However, this abruptly becomes different when scalar products are introduced – for normalisations, e.g.

A scalar product is a 1:1 mapping of an "**input**" vector V on an "**output**" vector V, thus doubling the number of vectors. In a different notation, such input vectors also are called "**creators**" and the output vectors "**destructors**". But this notation only makes sense as long as we might consider those vectors as being "**orthogonal**" to each other:

$$\langle \underline{\vec{e}}_j | \vec{e}_k \rangle = \begin{cases} 1 \text{ if } j{=}k, \\ 0 \text{ else} . \end{cases}$$

Vector pairs made of r- or c-numbers easily satisfy this condition. **Octonions** o replacing those e, on the other hand, only satisfy the upper condition (=1) (in fact, if e is just the inverse 1/e of e); the lower condition (=0), however, i.e., the freedom from zero divisors, will stay out of reach. *(This is because the norm of a product of octonions is equal to the product of their individual norms. Hence the product can vanish only if one of octonions vanishes.)*

Unless we are replacing

$$\vec{e}_i \ \rightarrow \ o_i \times \vec{e}_i .$$

In this case, however, we would throw out the octonion properties through the backdoor, leaving us with just their specific property **dimension = 8**, indeed. The crucial aspect of this argument is the property of a product output times input: Corresponding pairs, j=k, should be vastly superior to pairs j not equal to k not corresponding to each other. Last but not least, the latter should therefore be negligible with respect to the first ones, i.e., their measures should metrologically vanish "in practice".

Mathematicians refer to such a behaviour as that of a **zero divisor**: The product is vanishing although none of its individual factors does so. However, the hypercomplex numbers of dimension 8x8 = 64 are still waiting for their inspection with respect to their content of zero divisors and their mutual relations to each other. Surprising details in terms of orthogonal partial subsets which do suggest the above construction $o_i x e_i$ cannot yet be excluded. Actually, this problem has to be considered as still being open.

The group-theoretical point of view, however, looks quite different from its multiplicative one. From the point of view of a tensor product as a superposition of many Kronecker products, not the products but their commutators are relevant. While an elementary commutator will give rise to the result quoted above, the elementary, *micro*scopic commutator, after having been applied to all m Kronecker factors will give rise to the gross, *macro*scopic result

$$[\underline{e}_j, e_k] = m \, f_{jki} \, g_i \, .$$

(g is here a generator of the combined Lie algebra of all $\underline{e}$ and e.) Macroscopically, however, we are measuring the e, $\underline{e}$, and g in units of the magnitude m. Dividing by m squared, (with G = g/m, E = e/m, etc.) we obtain:

$$[\underline{E}_j, E_k] = \frac{1}{m^2} ([m\underline{E}_j, mE_k]) = \frac{1}{m^2} (f_{jki} \, mg_i) = \frac{1}{m}(f_{jki} \, G_i).$$

In the macroscopic limit m tending to infinity, this yields

$$[\underline{E}_j, E_k] = 0.$$

Since deSitter in the 1920s, this way of constructing a macroscopic limit is called **group contraction**.

Without being conscious of it, Einstein stopped this group contraction just before reaching its limit (radius of our universe tending to infinity). This provided his **curvilinear metric** f/m proportional to the inverse, almost infinite radius of curvature of our universe. (Without being conscious of it, he cancelled all higher approximations.)

Einstein did not (consciously) work with group theory. Therefore, he did not bother about an identification of the underlying group U(4,4). This made him overlook essential details: His General Relativity, hence, remained an incomplete patchwork; by passing its application area (restricted by those omissions) roughly wrong predictions are the result – the singularity behind his event horizon, e.g.

Now, we cannot work immediately by replacing those objects e by our **quanta** q because quanta will have to be conserved absolutely, and their number is tremendously big, i.e., in any case bigger than 8. When expressing their **individuality** by an additional label s (of an unknown range), we should formulate: QG is working with **classes** (types) of quanta:

$$\{q_a\} = (\{q_{a,s}\} \text{ modulus } \{s\}); \left\langle \vec{\underline{q}}_{j,r} \middle| \vec{\underline{q}}_{k,t} \right\rangle = \begin{cases} 1 \text{ if } (j,r) = (k,t), \\ 0 \text{ else.} \end{cases}$$

This (usually suppressed) notation in terms of classes occasionally will make QG somewhat nontransparent. On the other hand, it corresponds to the familiar tensor definition as a superposition of Kronecker products. Group contraction, first of all, will refer to the class logic of the s; its effect on the a (with s fixed) is subordinate. As the ranges of the partial s sets to be applied sometimes are not quite clear, normalisation problems arise. From time to time, hence, we shall have to use a somewhat vague, summarised formulation. In principle, however, everything is unique.

Classical quantum field theories, besides, often do not take the multiplication rules of their creation and destruction operators too seriously. They do not define them as "quanta". "2nd quantisation" does not strictly distinguish between a Kronecker product and an ordinary product when multiplying operators. As a result, in their "vacuum polarisation", a vacuum is not empty! Hence, it will not be surprising that a model that strongly ideologised has more blurred than promoted the understanding of fundamental physics for a century.

I already mentioned that deSitter and Dirac – both of them from different points of view – were close to detecting QG at their times, while Einstein, dazzled by his own development of General Relativity, was too much locked into the formalism of differential geometry and into his equivalence principle. Thus, he missed the breakthrough towards QG and to the "world formula", as well.

Let us forget about the actual literature on "Quantum Gravity". Like all quantum field theories, it does not work with General but with Special Relativity, i.e., exclusively with canonical quantisation. This has no relation to a "true" QG.

44. Problems Still Open in QG

The main problem of philosophy is: "Why is there **anything** at all?" The bulk of all further problems are of secondary order. Last but not least, the source, where its quanta are coming from, is unknown to QG, as well. QG only *works* with them and *organises* them according to our human senses: In case _that_ there is something, indeed, that something will have to be countable and finite – otherwise – as we demonstrated – a *Homo physicus* could not really "_understand_" it.

Hence, another fundamental problem of almost equal importance will read: "How far does a philosophical problem depend on **_human senses_**?"

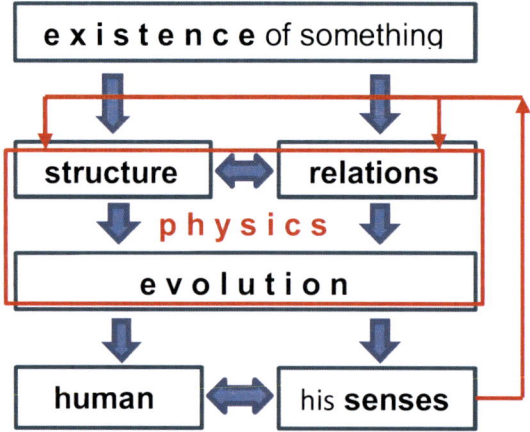

This recoupling of human senses to structure is a problem: Does this structure exist without involving human senses, as well – or how would that structure look like without it, respectively? Would it still be 8-dimensional? Is a normalised probability a subject of mankind or independent of him?

On the other hand, our 2-channel system will persist without humans, too. Zeilinger does his research with spin. Future faster-than-light technologies will extend it over spacetime, energy-momentum, and heavy mass, thus acting *across* our dynamic parity horizons.

By these extensions the technique that has become known as Einstein's "spooky action at a distance" (entanglement) is going to open the gate to totally novel technologies to come that nobody actually dares to dream of. Bell's superdeterminism makes it possible to rediagonalise the dynamic channel with its causality restrictions according to the velocity of light towards the reaction channel, which is free of them.

With his first fully operational computer, Konrad Zuse, in 1941 in Berlin, fired the starting gun for worldwide digitisation to control the subsequent century with its binary bit-up-bit-down architecture. After the steam engine at the end of the 19th century and the digitisation at the end of the 20th century, Quantum Gravity has a good chance to trigger the next technological revolution at the end of the 21st century.

The physical basics are on the table; everybody can serve himself – provided those actual "Luddites", dressed up as a dyed-in-the-wool conservative administrators, do not remain in charge to continue preventing any progress in fundamental theory by virtue of office (official publication monopole), an administration which at all costs is only bent on keeping its old, worn-out privileges (rankings, hereditary publication rights, etc.).

The next pending tasks could be the explicit calculation of all sorts of **transition amplitudes** for selected particle reactions **on a numerical baseline** in order, first of all, to get the experimental experience for, then, dealing with more complicated processes based on the shell model to replace the spin-statistics theorem outdated long since.

In parallel, cosmology will have to be whipped into shape by QG. Especially, an update is urgently needed with respect to the consequences resulting from the world formula including its higher Casimir operators (for completing Einstein's metric and including dark energy and dark matter, e.g.). Black holes, parities, and horizons of all types need that _consistent_ treatment provided by QG.

Actually, transition amplitudes, essentially, address those 8 static _charges_ only, considering them as the octet counterparts of the "internal" singlet "particle number". Just incidentally, in 2013, I mentioned their rediagonalisation to give rise to those hadronic flavours (which I depicted in various colours, above), in the scope of a lecture [8]. The answer to the "why" and to the principle leading to this rediadonalisation remained vague, so far. Its need and form will presumably be related to that special split off of dark matter. This means a hint towards the microscopic realisation of the higher Casimirs by Dirac's formalism.

Especially for electrodynamics, besides this **electric charge Q**, only its **4-potential A** is actually fixed to be the octet counterpart of the linear **4-momentum P**; the $\underline{A}$ corresponding to the 4 components of "**electromagnetic spacetime**" is still ignored. The gauge of A got stuck in preliminaries. The summary of electromagnetic features under some superior, general-relativistic field tensor F_{ab} is missing completely.

But this is just _one_ of those points still to be clarified by experiment, especially for electrodynamics. In addition, however, there are still 7 more "internal" octet potentials representing counterparts of that singlet energy-momentum. The SM speculates to and fro by applying its variational principle, which, with its arbitrarily assumed Lagrange components considered to represent "strong" interactions (i.e., triality T), is unapt for QG and leaving open the parts of the additional potentials A and M.

For "weak" interactions, by its W- and Z-mesons, the SM even restricts itself to a mere dipole ansatz, thus ignoring the monopole charge Λ, which is the main part of the "weak" nuclear power. Hence, forget about the remaining forces! (But which cosmic effects will those charges N, L, A, M provoke due to their range horizons that are not restricted to a microscopic scope?)

And what is the physical significance the 8 octet variants of the Lorentz booster, and what is that of heavy mass?? A lot of open questions. For experimental physicists, this means the start of a golden age of important discoveries never considered before. By its clearly formulated world formula, QG opened totally new horizons for cosmology, as well. Let us stop grumpily sticking our heads in the sand! Let us pick up the great challenges of the age: Physics will hardly offer such an opportunity another time!

Isn't it curious that the antiparticles we are experimenting with are identified to represent objects allocated **behind the event horizon**? (Cf. the sketches of Chapter 19.) Hence electrons and nuclei are separated by the event horizon! Only their <u>spacetime projections</u> sometimes happen to coincide with each other. Then they are able to build up compound structures like atoms, molecules, mountains, and galaxies.

The **matryoshka** principle even opens the gate towards quite different **levels** of consciousness ranging far beyond our daily duties of quanta and universes, which sandwich the macroscopic world we are a part of. The mater-mundi principle, however, demonstrates that those strange areas, as abstract as they might look at first glance, are not objects of merely philosophical speculation. They do strongly interact with our daily life in terms of the "internal" forces like electromagnetism, e.g.! In physics, everything is related to everything: Boundaries are just approximations that neglect something in order not to lose sight of the basic objectives.

A problem still open is "**How many quanta of which type** are attributed to **our universe**?" This, however, is no problem of theory but a problem to be measured and counted by experiment. Theory, then, *relates* those 64 counts to the strength and to the dynamic [an]isotropy of the 8 "internal" forces then to be cross-checked by experiment, again.

Another especially important problem still open is: Which **particle**, now, really *is* **massive** and which one is **massless** – and why?

Another problem still open is one of statistical relevance: According to which principle are those **non-valence bricks distributed** to the various, particular **"stable" particle** types? This is closely connected to the problem of the **spectrum of stable particles**. And this is a matter of Bell's consistency principle (his superdeterminism).

The Story

II-1. First Contact

On a lovely summer day in the the late 1950s, at noon. Next to the final stop of my tram in the city of Tegel (Berlin), there was a busy newsstand. From far away already, on my way home from school, a huge headline attracted my attention: "**World Formula … Heisenberg**". It took some time until Heisenberg's error had been disproved. My interest, however, had been activated – although my school notes in physics were bad: That non-ending "If you pull here, you get an effect there" of school physics had bored me to death.

During my preparations for the first university examination in physics (the German "Vordiplom", similar to a "bachelor") I tried to get some systematic insight into all those diverging models that had been offered in the lessons before.

This was the time when the **Berlin wall** was going to be erected. Thereafter, an increasing fear went through the town that the Russians might take it over. Professors took to their heels "escaping" towards the west. That, however, needed an appointment elsewhere, retarding their exodus somewhat.

After finishing my lessons, internships, compulsory seminars, etc., I saw the last professor of theoretical physics still left in office and asked him for the admission to start work at some master thesis (German "Diplom"). He principally agreed but advised me first to buy a certain book of 1.000 pages narrowly printed with formulas on the theories of particle physics. After having understood all that I would have to present myself again.

Thus, I kept learning day and night all around the clock. Then I asked him again. In the meantime, however, he had been offered a professorship in the west. He asked me to follow him there. In my juvenile blindness, I told myself: If one professor is going, another one soon will be taking over his job; two newcomers had been announced, already.

Half a year later, the first of them arrived, indeed. He brought along a couple of PhD students from his former university. But to my own question, he told me that he did not yet have the titles for a thesis because he had taken over the job of a professor too recently; I should wait. Now, as a diploma student, however, I got access to the institute and to its special library – but I was advised to wait. Thus, I studied the actual journals and the flood of preprints coming in from all over the world, but I was doomed to wait, wait, and wait – for years as it turned out!

II-2. Starting Work

This was the golden epoch when **Gell-Mann** launched his "Eightfold Way" on "SU(3)" and his **quarks**. Hence, I familiarised myself with the mathematical discipline of "**group theory**" treating that subject. Especially, S. Okubo's preprints on SU(3) mass formulas and **Casimir** operators attracted my interest.

Then, Gell-Mann's SU(3)-formalism of "*internal*" parameters (iso-spin, electric charge, etc.) were extended by the factor 2 of the *dynamic* dimension of spin giving an "SU(6)". **W. Rühl**, shortly afterwards, extended that SU(6) towards an "SL(6,c)" by boosting the spin formalism to a complete Lorentz behaviour, which **Abdus Salam**, finally, extended to an SU(12) by still incorporating **Dirac's** 4-dimensional formalism into Gell-Mann's 3-dimensional quark system.

After years of waiting, waiting and waiting, the 2nd professor of theoretical physics who had been announced years ago entered the stage, but immediately left it again. The official justification was that his obligations had required him to stay at Hamburg for another year in order to finish his works, there.

Then, he arrived, indeed, bringing along a post-doc from Hamburg. Angry about the previous long waiting period with the other professor, I straight away switched over to him, tempting him by the statement that, meanwhile, I myself had found a title for a thesis: "Modified SU(6) mass formulas". He agreed and I started my work.

During all the time I was writing my thesis, however, I had *not a single contact* with my professor about my thesis. Hence, there neither was no way to direct his attention towards that obvious offence to all didactics which, according to my understanding, consisted in that *jumble* of classical methods of applying <u>continuous</u> *functional analysis* to the <u>discrete</u> models based on (the "eigenvalues" of) *group theory*.

155

Instead of properly solving the problem within the framework of *one* of the mathematical disciplines, people let themselves be diverted to switch over to another one that did not get that problem under control, either. Thus, all those urgent problems still standing never went to be solved but just became suspended towards a day never to come. "Goulash physics" was reigning: Just take a piece of everything and stir the mixture.

All my senses were directed to properly eliminating those ancient, functional-analytic "impurities" from those new, group-theoretical models! According to my conviction this would be the only chance to **reconcile Einstein's world** with **Planck's quanta** and **Gell-Mann's quarks**.

This primarily meant reducing that double dependence of Dirac's basic components – on the one hand on discrete *labels*, on the other hand on additional, continuous *arguments* – towards some basis purely consisting of discrete labels. My motto, thus, was: "No arguments".

Hence, I had to make dynamics discrete as well. Spin had been the starting option. But how could I treat momentum and spacetime the same way? The quantum aspect of Dirac's 4 components had been identified long since by writing them down in terms of a formalism ("2nd quantization") of "creation" and "destruction" operators. I changed the name to "**quanta**".

In order to transform the continuous spectra of dynamics into discrete spectra, my appropriate trick was to express those "argument values" by "numbers of quanta" (of whatsoever sort). This shifted the continuity problem over to the **statistics** of (various types of) discrete quanta.

At that time, the state of all these reflections was still underdeveloped. Especially, I still had no idea which the final transformation *group* might be to manage all that. For a long time, I vainly turned that problem over and over in my mind – and wasted a lot of scratch paper. Einstein's works were not helpful, either.

Another shortcoming of Gell-Mann's disciples has been their bottom-up access to group theory by integrating infinitesimal transformations according to functional analysis, thus confining themselves to "simple" groups, i.e., to those "special" ($\underline{S}$U(...) and $\underline{S}$O(...)) groups neglecting **particle number**, **electric charge**, etc. This way, they *could not* find a concise model satisfying the challenges of a New Physics!

Due to having noticed that conceptual deficit right from the beginning, I myself preferred to apply A. **Young's top-down access** leading to the full (U(...) and O(...)) groups which included the respective linear Casimir operators. Thus, it was not a surprise for me, when people later on continued to **ignore** the higher **Casimir operators**, as well. Remember, however, that **Einstein's bent metric**, **dark energy**, and **dark matter**, i.e., major problems of cosmology, all result from the **world formula** based on higher-order Casimirs!

My contact person concerning my thesis exclusively was that post-doc stuffing one slab of chocolate after the other into his mouth. His standard answer to every question was: "Just try it". No more. A few months after my successful **graduation**, he unexpectedly died.

Because my professor was the only person in the institute who still distributed scientific studies, I had applied him for a PhD position before already. Thus, I got the job of a scientific **assistant** at the institute. But again, my only contact with him, this time in his position of the supervisor of my thesis, was about my work in my position as a scientific assistant (designing and executing the student's training, recording examinations, etc.). (The seminars had been organised by the other professor.)

II-3. Assistance

Due to the shortage of professors as a long-term result of that Berlin wall, the city announced a university reform. Briefly: Everybody who already had a doctor's degree, was employed and gave lessons, there, at some later key date was promised promotion to become an "assistant-professor" paid by the city administration.

Hence, people from everywhere rushed to Berlin. My institute welcomed a new post-doc arriving from the United States, specialised on group theory, i.e., exactly on my special subject! Hence, I again switched over, this time in order to do my doctorate. During my long waiting periods in the position of a PhD student, I had collected enough independent knowledge. Thus, I hoped finally to end that vicious circle of an unsatisfactory waiting period in favour of some truly scientific interaction with competent partners.

My idea had been to free Gell-Mann's "**Standard Model**" from all its inconsistent and unnecessary admixtures of functional analysis by generating some model self-consistent in pure group theory. Primarily that meant not only to express those "internal" parameters in terms of discrete labels but to "digitise" dynamics as well. My "quanta" represented my starting option.

At that time, I did not yet care about Bell's no-go theorems. I considered my task simply to be that of finding a *pragmatic solution*, *whatever it might look like*. Perhaps, you have heard of that maverick slogan: "Everybody said: That does not work. Then, there was somebody who did not know that. He did it."

By combining and recombining my "quanta" with each other, I soon verified *why* there was no exact microscopic solution within a finite representation. The way out, inevitably needed the *macroscopic* approach by **statistics**. Statistics, however, meant a superposition of <u>many</u> distinguishable states. With *discrete* quanta, this necessarily meant that a *multitude* of quanta should be present simultaneously.

Hence, in spite of their similarity, "quanta" could not any more be Gell-Mann's "quarks"! His "standard" model rigorously postulated that an elementary particle should consist of 3 quarks at most. Here again, the premature decision of a few "top dogs" powerfully blocked the productive research of generations to come; authoritarianism was the ruling key concept!

My new supervisor from the Middle West did not show much interest in physics. His skills ranged more in – I would call it – sales promotion: Publishing was his first target, no matter what – the *number* of (his) own publications was it what counted, and nothing else. Thus, I quickly learned that I should keep my intermediate results under lock and key as long as I had not completely finished them. Again, the university had proved not to be an appropriate place to discuss scientific ideas.

Hence, it just was a matter of time before I had to quit that institution. My idea in the direction of unifying Einstein's General Relativity with Planck's idea of quanta to give rise to a Quantum Gravity (QG) in terms of a pure group theory had no chance of realisation inside a university just riding on the *traditional*, functional-analytic pathways of fundamental physics and defending it tooth and nail.

The longer I argued and puzzled about it, the clearer it became to me from month to month: The nuts and bolts of a QG, this was the **quantisation of Einstein's *General* Relativity**. Without it, nothing would proceed on that field at all! All the rest which, later on, would be designated as a "QG", *was* no QG – it only would have misused that name.

The formal indication of having overcome those traditional dead-end models of that outdated functional analysis in terms of a quantum field theory whatever it might look like, was it – consciously and intentionally, to perform the break with canonical quantisation, i.e., to reproduce Einstein's metric tensor.

At the CERN, at Geneva, I quickly learned how people formally managed to raise the number of their publications by joining their forces in terms of "collaborations" and mutual quotations. My new boss had introduced me to some fellows (post-docs) from Italy and Portugal amusing themselves with "tilt" angles – which, according to my opinion, was no more than an occupational therapy without any physical background. But CERN staff members may publish a lot …

At the institute's library, I also used my long waiting periods in order to look through the old articles published between the two World Wars. There, I happened to run into **deSitter**'s formalism of "**group contraction**": He had succeeded in gaining the dynamic Poincaré group out of a 5-dimensional rotation group by applying some limiting process.

My conclusion was that, in Quantum Gravity, that contraction process should have to be stopped <u>before</u> reaching its limit. One of its yields was an extreme, but still finite normalisation for momentum and spacetime, another one some **metric** à la Einstein's GR: a fantastic result for my own model! Without having been conscious of it, I had thus detected in the early 1970s what, later on, would give rise to the new definition of what should be considered as "macroscopic" when following Bell's 1985 superdeterminism!

Besides statistics, hence, that contraction process still should be applied there, in addition to which, however, it should be stopped before reaching its limit. Furthermore – and that, too, was my own idea in order to get over deSitter's deadlock situation: Einstein's variant of a *non-linear spacetime* would have to be transformed into the **linear CMS-spacetime**.

Thus, at the end of my university career, I almost had QG under control, already. My original hope, however, to habilitate in QG – after branching off the quantisation of Einstein's curvilinear spacetime, before, in order to use it for a doctorate – had been dashed by the expiration of my last temporary contract at my university – simply because I had *not* succeeded *in time* to reach the final end of my ambitious research.

I had used my position to renew and prolong my temporary contracts as often as possible in order to maintain access to the institute's literature. After 7 semesters of working as a scientific assistant, I left that free research life in order to earn my money with a major industry, where fundamental physics was no subject any more for the decades to come.

II-4. Late Success

As a recipient of a retirement pension, I remembered my hoary findings from university, reviewed my notices, arranged them, and submitted the quantisation of Einstein's bent spacetime to the New Journal of Physics in London in 2006. There, it successfully passed the peer review and was released for publication.

Then, however, I got another e-mail telling me that I had forgotten to indicate my full **address** – please register with the form enclosed. Here, "address" essentially meant the triple

- academic title (only Prof. and Dr. admitted),
- institution (i.e., university or institute),
- sponsor.

My 3-fold response: not applicable. The prompt answer by machine read: Publication rejected. This, hence, was the praised "freedom of research" of the 21st century: a step back into the darkest Middle Ages, feudalism at its "finest"! Actually, the scientific substance of a text confirmed by a peer review was not the decisive criterion for being published, but the "noble" descent (address) of the author: **Descent had priority over substance!**

Highest priority has the economic value the publication can be assigned to by an institution's ranking – the scientific impact is of minor importance. At once, it became totally obvious to me how it could have happened that those notorious "string models" managed for decades to control the theoretical literature on fundamental physics preventing *theory* from proceeding, although they demonstrably had no relevance to physics at all.

Those economic considerations have been the reason that fundamental research on its *theoretical* part has been lagging behind for a century already. Einstein and Schrödinger, as the icons of times long since gone by, are simply sacrosanct. Even today, nobody seriously dares to come up with doubts nor *sincerely* to discuss alternatives.

From the CERN to Harvard, Princeton, and Stanford, there are complete "armies" marching on the wrong track, meanwhile – without having any chance to advance fundamental physics a little step forward. The old guard is simply practising those tools (functional analysis) it grew up with, and the junior staff is hyperventilating with superman esotericisms like the string models, far beyond physics. Common to both groups is their inability to agree on pragmatic compromises. Inbreeding as their program!

On the other side, there are those prejudices which, by economic reasoning, do not admit sufficient time for developing well-thought-out ideas, are always prepared to turn off their money supply, demanding quick ad-hoc solutions without sustainability. According to this American method, a Gordian knot will never be tediously solved but cut by brute force. The disastrous consequences of such an act of barbarious destruction are not considered – cf. "2nd quantisation", cf. that "3-quarks-only" postulate, cf. the variational principle, cf. the spin-statistics theorem, etc., etc. Research funds, thus, are for experiment, not for theory!

Finally, there still are those fundamentalists that do not allow any fact to divert them from their ivory-tower fantasies. Their simple Trump-like policy reads: "Theory is correct, nature is wrong". This, obviously, is the category that string models belong to, which even by the most serious contradictions of their "theories" towards experiment stick to their guns: Their institution will back everything. And those incurable symmetry fans tend in the same direction, as well.

Some sound shift of paradigms is needed: Hands off the bureaucratic fetishism of accidental *curriculum*s, acknowledge the power of models to *describe* *nature* as it is!

While the string fans keep on trying to persuade nature to act in a way it definitely does *not* do, the implications of the model presented here, as far as they are already verifiable, are fully in accordance with nature from the beginning. Moreover, a deep understanding of how nature works is, indeed, its result.

II-5. Life Goes On

Thus, I pondered my next actions. Should I resign? No, I couldn't: my head still was full of ideas not yet implemented. There was that "**quark confinement**", e.g., whose solution I had ready – that experimental fact that Gell-Mann's quarks exclusively appeared in triads, which the official literature was unable to explain.

I had found the **GUT** and **ToE** mechanism according to which the set of all those separate, **chiral forces** of nature allowed for unification under one single, common concept. Etc., etc. Thus, I collected some still longer series of new results found in the meantime and deposited them in 2010 as a print-book [1] (in the German language) at the Leipzig and Frankfurt sites of the German National Library.

Another result was that there are no symmetries in nature. In literature, all those symmetries called for had to be "broken": nature is not even rotationally invariant, e.g.; daily life disproves it! "Symmetry groups", hence, will have to be replaced by "classification groups". By mathematics, such a "**classification**" is not achieved by complete transformation groups but, more subtly, by their "**generators**" as collected in their "**Lie-algebras**", already.

That mixing of alleged "symmetries" and really conserved quantities (by misusing **Noether's theorem**) has meanwhile reached such a state of gobbledygook and half-truths (like "broken quantum numbers") that even hard-core specialists are hardly aware any more of the fact that all that is *not* generally applicable to statistical superpositions of partial representations.

Hardly had I deposited my records when I happened to come across a notice on the properties of **octonion** numbers. This observation, then, became the key to settling the dimension problem for my model, which, up to then, only had been 4x8-dimensional in the 2 channels. Hence, I prepared myself to communicate these finding

165

at the annual spring conferences organised by the German Physical Community (DPG).

After having found a publisher, I released my first e-book in the English language in 2013 [2], beside its German version. The problem, however, was: If in QG everything was fixed – how, then, could there be any **motion**? This problem was solved in my next e-book [3] in 2014. My subsequent focus switched over to **black-hole dynamics**.

It is based on the **3 parities**, especially on **charge-conjugation** parity. Its doubling of Einstein's 4 dimensions to 8 is the key to understanding black holes as equivalent structures in competition to our own world. Contrary to conventional wisdom, the world **behind the event horizon** revealed itself to be of a totally **equivalent structure** as "our" world in front of it! And – even more difficult to accept – this event horizon, being neutralised by the Lorentz horizon, extends right between an atomic nucleus and its electron shell!

Thus, I accumulated my notices accrued in the meantime to release the first **textbook of Quantum Gravity** [4] to exist in the world, which treated the details of QG. For comparison: In the official literature, many books are published in the name of QG. However, all of them just end up by telling the reader that QG had *not* yet been found and that it still would need decades to detect it. My own textbook even describes the dynamics of black holes explicitly, in a consistent way free of singularities. Hawking could only dream of it!

As another world premiere, I released the first explicit calculation of the **fine-structure constant** (electric charge), there. My subsequent years were dedicated to **Bell**'s no-go theorems and his **superdeterminism**, which I myself had pragmatically applied long since in terms of my 2-channel system without having been conscious of that background [5] [6] – a consistent description of nature just needed it in this way.

In the official literature, again and again I meet those incredible simplifications and deadly misunderstandings contradicting nature – and the media, faithfully believing in "science", uncritically propagate that nonsense.

Endlessly, those tired, old devotions to false statements and to so-called still unexplainable facts I had resolved and published long since appear on domestic television monitors. It is hard not to have any effective opportunity to shout into those untidy nurseries: "Hombre, _there_ is your mistake, this and that must be changed if it should work!"

While political journals live on the alternatives intruding from all directions, scientific newspapers doggedly renounce all opposition; the silence of death is the brand spread over "science". Physical laws are not _detected_ anymore but _passed_ by acclamation. As if hypnotised, even experienced "science journalists" uncritically swallow all that official institutes offer, like rabbits fixated by a snake, ignoring the fact that those institutions are following their own strategy.

The prime discipline of journalistic research, i.e., duly to involve opposing aspects and critics, is tacitly swept under the carpet by those "scientific" reports – especially on the sector of the theory of fundamental physics. By their systematic refusal to comply with their objective duty of neutrality, those science "journalists", actually, are denying their professional ethics in favour of cheap effects!

As placebos, then, those Korean falsifications of statistics and that carelessness in quoting statements is denounced political opponents are blamed with. Those considerably more serious failures in particle theory and in cosmology, however, have been tacitly accepted for almost a century. George Orwell's novels "Animal Farm" and "1984" (making "New-Speak" a subject) are celebrating an alarming revival.

My following e-book [7] supplements the **matryoshka** and **mater-mundi principles**. In addition, **Pauli's exclusion principle** is derived from the "internal" parameters by using the shell models at the expense of the semi-classical spin-statistics theorem. This, again, opens new horizons to understanding how nature works.

For example, there is that accelerated extension of our universe by dark energy. By QG, this is some formal result of the mutual **rejection** of its quanta triggered by their density gradient. **Dark energy**, hence, is nothing other than quite an ordinary **entropy effect**! On the other hand, **attraction** by **gravity** is just an oppositely directed special effect of this entropic force when applied to extended bodies in a layered medium (**quantum density**). Einstein's **geometrisation** of gravity, hence, implicitly extends to <u>all</u> 8 fundamental forces of nature. Or consider the **shear effect** from the reaction to the dynamic channel: Its contribution to the **event horizon** is the **admixture of heavy mass to CMS-time**, pretending the existence of another, **2nd time,** etc.

The present text may be considered as a largely extended remake of my last e-book [7] to clarify additional relations that have not yet been sufficiently in focus.

Meanwhile, official literature continues its dice games with continuous, special-relativistic functional analysis, wasting its time with renormalisation, string-brane, and want-to-be QG models – tightly keeping its eyes shut towards a true quantisation of Einstein's curvilinear spacetime. Contrary to the situation in the official vicinity of those functional-analysists showing little true, lasting innovation for 100 years, now, there is considerable progress off the stage (see above). Only the official literature tightly barricades itself against progress in order to keep dozing on together with those string dreamers. Go to sleep on, physics, peacefully, go to sleep on!

II-6. "Science"

The start of non-classical physics can be fixed in the year 1900, when, at Berlin, the physicist **Planck** quantised black-body radiation ("Planck constant") and, at Cambridge, the mathematician A. Young released his top-down version of group theory (notions: "**Young tableaux**", "**irreducibility**"). Later on, in 1905 and 1915, **Einstein** followed with his relativity theories, and in 1926 the electron **spin** was detected. Before those times, functional-analytic methods had dominated theoretical physics.

As usual, a revolution already contains the seed of its counter-revolution. Physicists who grew up with functional analysis heavily obstructed group-theoretical methods that they had not learned in their university curriculum. Especially severe was that hostile objection to novel ideas in the old Habsburgian bureaucracy in Austria: Pauli and Schrödinger even went hawking with their defaming notion of what they called "**group pestilence**".

In this poisoned atmosphere, the Dutch astronomer **deSitter** was developing his astronomic models applying "**group contraction**". As a child of his century, however, deSitter failed to consider *stopping* that contraction process before reaching its limit. Thus, deSitter failed to discover (one of) the most important entry points to QG at the last moment. I discussed **Dirac**'s entry point already, where he had failed to extend his 4 to all 16 gamma-matrices. Entry #3 is **Bell**'s superdeterminism substantiating what is "macroscopic" and the channel split (reaction vs. dynamic channel).

That "group pestilence" reflected the uneasiness of a major part of professors towards that new trend of unfamiliar mathematics in physics. Everybody prayed for its end and tried to survive that gap of knowledge as long as that trend still endured by unswervingly continuing his application of the old functional-analytic methods, ignoring group theory as long as possible. This, of course, was the worst thing that could happen to a theory.

Quantum theories were hence left to Schrödinger, who was happy to avert the pending Damocles' sword of modern physics towards a mere introduction of Planck's constant into the old variational principle. And Pauli managed the spin=1/2 problem by inventing his 4 Pauli matrices. But this was not really a solution to the new challenges posed by quantum theories.

Einstein effectively retired from active physics by bathing in the sun of his glory. He didn't even try to extend his General Relativity by spin or to present it in a form treating spacetime and energy-momentum on some equal footing. He only tried – in vain – to merge General Relativity with electrodynamics and pondered – again without success – what his "world formula" might look like. Without applying the notion of "irreducibility" (Casimir operators), however, he had no chance.

In those years, the course of the decades to come had been set. In order to improve quality, in that nameless country between Canada and the United States of Mexico, the **peer review** for scientific publications came into vogue driving Einstein up the wall.

After World War II, that peer review degenerated from its initial purpose of guaranteeing quality into a commercial tool of mere economic competition among the leading scientific institutions and organisations. Thus, it shared its "value" left with the declining reputation of a doctor's title. In many cases, both of them had been distributed to satisfy economic or social, political codes of conduct – and increasingly less to scientific excellence.

Actually, a peer review is not any more the admission ticket for a scientific publication it once had been designed for, but it is handled as a tiresome appendix to what collectively is called an "address" (title, institution, sponsor). This "address" is the crucial point a publisher uses to decide by if a publication will offer enough lasting profit for his journal – or not. The (secondary) peer review just turned to some annoying duty not taken too seriously.

This explains why the SM, as time went by, could accumulate such a vast multitude of inconsistent entries, half-truths, and singularities that even the expert will hardly have enough time to keep track of its twists and turns. Hence, resistance faded away over time, giving rise to a ubiquitous resignation ever to find a way out of that impenetrable jungle.

At the expense of real science, leading institutions meanwhile enjoy some rather dictatorial jester's licence, when they can specify by closed-shop regulations what "the world" will have to "believe". Incredible the methods theoreticians are able to resort to as long as nobody is prepared to control them!

On the other hand, everybody is absolutely sure that what the present state-of-the-art fundamental theory has achieved in terms of the SM *cannot* be true! In my e-books, I addressed the most spectacular errors of the last 100 years. QG, as presented, until down to the derivation of the correct value of the fine-structure constant, where many of the special details of QG enter, strictly avoids the repetition of those errors radically erased.

The experimental confirmation of QG as far as it has been tested already is evidence for a promising future of fundamental theory – as soon as the generation of those wise guys of functional analysis retires. Popular textbook features like the spin-statistics theorem based on semi-classical superstition and solicitation will have to be abandoned; the higher principle of Young's irreducibility should gain more attention among physicists. I do not want to talk, here, about those "string" alchemists arguing completely beyond physics.

But Dirac, too, got on the wrong track with his "2nd quantisation". Nevertheless, it was his merit, together with Feynman's, thus to have made popular the notion of "virtual" states totally absent in Einstein's works. QG is ordering that chaos, re-placing all that to its correct position.

In a word: Scientists are humans, as well – with all of their short-comings. Their public glorification in the media is **counterproductive**. Especially in stagnating fields, the yield will be the dogmatic arro-gance of self-proclaimed "Illuminati fraternities" doggedly defend-ing their **misconceptions**.

A 6-digit number of sold copies of my German and English e-books on Quantum Gravity and New Physics – those warez versions not even added – support the unbroken expectation of the younger generation in universities still to trust in a potential "understanding" of fundamental physics by theory. Do not let us disappoint them again!

Footnotes

Historical textbook subjects and names are not especially quoted. For the layman, those quotes can easily be looked up on the internet. Especially for Quantum Gravity and New Physics, their temporal development is found under www.q-grav.com.

[1] C. Birkholz, "Weltbild *nach Vereinheitlichung aller Kräfte der Natur ...*", Selbstverlag (2010), ISBN 978-3-00-030847-6

[2] C. Birkholz, "New Physics", bookrix/München (2013).

[3] C. Birkholz, "Flow of Time", bookrix/München (2014).

[4] C. Birkholz, "**ToE; New Physics explaining our world by Quantum Gravity**. *World's first textbook on QG*", an e-book by Bookrix, Munich (2016).

[5] C. Birkholz, "Cognition based on Quantum Gravity", bookrix/München (2016).

[6] C. Birkholz, "Where Einstein had failed", bookrix/München (2017).

[7] C. Birkholz, "Dirac topping Einstein", bookrix/München (2019).

[8] C. Birkholz, Lecture AGPhil 10.3 „Successfully Unravelling the Structure of Our Universe and Its Particles by First Principles", DPG Spring Conf. on Grav., Jena/Germany (2013). See www.q-grav.com.